ROSE SWEET

Dear God, SEND ME A SOUL MATE

Eight steps for finding a spouse... God's way

AMG
Publishers

God's Word is our highest calling.

Dear God, Send Me a Soul Mate
Copyright © 2002 by Rose Sweet

Published by AMG Publishers
6815 Shallowford Rd.
Chattanooga, Tennessee 37421

ISBN 0-89957-357-6

First printing—July 2002

Cover designed by Phillip Rodgers, AMG Publishers
Interior design and typesetting by Reider Publishing Services,
San Francisco, California
Edited and Proofread by Judy Bodmer, Gwen Waller, Dan
Penwell, and Jody El-Assadi

Printed in Canada
 08 07 06 05 04 03 02 –T– 8 7 6 5 4 3 2

Contents

Foreword

*W*hat does a long-dead, French mathematician have to do with finding your soul mate?

Georges Comte de Buffon, a young aristocratic genius born in 1707 was only twenty years old when he discovered the binomial theorem (whatever that is?). My research on the Internet shows that he is most remembered in mathematics for a probability experiment in which he calculated *pi* by throwing sticks over his shoulder onto a tiled floor and counting the number of times the sticks fell across the lines between the tiles. The poor guy kept trying over and over to get the right result. Sounds terribly mundane, repetitive, and frustrating—like the singles dating scene.

Georges Buffon's experiment stimulated scientific discussions and further discovery about understanding probability. Today you might want to know what the probability is that you will *ever* find your soul mate. Like Buffon, you may be spending what seems like an eternity waiting for the result you want. *When will my soul mate arrive? Where will I find him or her? Will this person be "The One?"*

Well, Buffon gives us wise advice. Smart scientists have always known that God is in the equation, and that He is waiting patiently for us to discover His hand in things. So in your search for a soul mate, never doubt that even in this numbers game of love and romance God's delays are not God's denials.

* * *

"Never think that God's delays are God's denials. Hold on; hold fast; hold out. Patience is genius."—Georges Louis-Leclerc, Comte de Buffon (1707–1788)

Acknowledgments

*I*f a soul mate is one who shares your dream and helps you achieve it, then I had help from the best of soul mates in the writing of this book:

Dan Penwell, hardworking editor and AMG Publisher's Manager of New Product Development, who passionately shares in my vision to light a fire in the reader's heart;

Judy Bodmer, Gwen Waller, and Jody El-Assadi, editors and perfectionists whose red pens polished my words to a bright shine;

Fred and Florence Littauer and all the CLASS (Christian Leaders, Authors, & Speakers Services) staff who play wonderful matchmakers in marrying writers with the best publishers;

All the young and old, single, married, or divorced men and women who opened their hearts and allowed me to use their stories of longing for love;

My friends, family, and especially my "boys," Mike and Joe, who someday will be looking for *their* soul mate.

You are all loved and deeply appreciated.

Introduction

"There's something *very* mysterious about him," confided my girlfriend between bites of her curried shrimp salad. Shirley and I were enjoying a late afternoon lunch on the pretty vine-covered patio at Tommy Bahama's Restaurant, and she was describing the man with whom she was trying to fix me up.

"Like what?" I asked, slowly stirring my iced tea. My friends were always intent on playing matchmaker, and Shirley was no exception.

"Well," Shirley said, "He was raised on the islands, and I think his parents were royalty or something."

"Yeah, right," I rolled my eyes.

"He doesn't have any kids, but he's got a lot of money. We've known him for years and, he's not only the nicest guy, he's smart. Somebody needs to snag him. He's got a huge mansion, an expensive car, and I think he works for a secret government agency. He may even be a spy!"

"Oh, for crying out loud, Shirley!" I spat out in disbelief, shaking my head.

Shirley pursed her lips and glared at me. I knew that my matchmaker friend would not give up until I gave in.

"Okay," I said, "*Okay!* I'll go out with him. Shee-sh!"

Then I smiled. "I admit I like the royalty part, and the rich thing is cool, but honey, let's get down to what's really important. Can the guy keep up with me *eight hours in a mall?*"

Shirley's shrimp flew out of her mouth, and we both howled with laughter so loud that our waiter jumped, dropping the dessert tray. While the poor guy was wiping up whipped cream, Shirley and I raised our glasses, clinked, and toasted to serious shoppers everywhere.

* * *

I did go out with Secret Agent Man, but it was a disaster, as usual. He was dull, boring, and could barely carry on a conversation. His pants were too short, his hair was too long, and he smelled like he'd washed his clothes in bacon fat. We had nothing in common, and I am trying to be kind in describing him as slightly, well, ugly. When he picked me up for our date, I wanted to cry, scream, and run away, but I knew that Shirley would never forgive me.

Since I've been divorced, my friends feel obliged to marry me off, so I can better fit into their social circles. I admit, in the past I've asked them to help me find a nice man. I've since learned two important things:

(1) I want a lot more than just "nice." My list is very specific.

(2) Whoever assists my search for a soul mate needs to know me, understand what I need and want, and not be compelled to match me with just anyone. They also need to understand what God wants for me.

We're Doing It All Wrong

Have you ever gone to dating school? Neither have I. No one ever taught me the right way to date or the right things to look for in a mate. I learned about dating and relationships from television, movies, magazines, and those foolish romance novels. Guys usually learn about dating in the proverbial locker room, not a place most distinguished for its wise counselors. Looking back, everything I ever tried ultimately failed. As a result, I have made poor choices in partners and had my heart broken more times than I care to count. I also have deeply hurt some very good men.

If you're like me, the older you get, the smarter you hope to become. A few years ago, I celebrated a significant birthday and realized that my life thus far had not fulfilled my dreams as a young woman. Up to that point, I'd tried doing everything my way, or the way my friends or those magazines told me, and I finally had to admit it wasn't working. In fact, it had never worked! Then as I looked around at the unhappy relationships, unfaithful marriages, and high rate of divorce, I realized that many were failing miserably or doomed to fail somewhere down the road.

Something inside me clicked that year. I felt sick of doing the same thing over and over and expecting different results. I was ready for something new. Thankfully, I have a loving God. When I'd had enough of failed relationships and heartache and was finally ready to listen, He gently tapped me on the shoulder and pointed me to a precious gift He'd given long ago—His Word. Scripture offers direction and wisdom for every problem in the world— every obstacle, even how to date and how to find your soul mate.

That's when I read the Old Testament story of Isaac and Rebecca with new insight. Isaac wanted a soul mate, and God brought him the perfect partner. If God did that then, why couldn't He do that now? Couldn't He bring *me* the right mate?

You and I Are Not Alone

I frequently speak to teens, and I also run a DivorceCare group in my city. Week after week, I hear the stories of men and women, young and old, never married or recently divorced, who desperately long for a soul mate. So I decided to send out a "Soul-Mate Survey" to see what people were looking for and just how they thought they were going to find it. Some of their answers surprised me because, despite their age, education, or experience, many remain incredibly naïve. No wonder the divorce rate keeps skyrocketing. This book grew out of their stories and my own experiences of looking for love.

Perhaps you're ready to throw in the towel on dating. Maybe your head is spinning with the dating-waiting-dating-waiting-dating game, and you want to climb off the carousel. Are you ready for something new? Do you want to find the perfect partner? Help is here. God is still the Almighty—He can move heaven and earth. But right now I have a much smaller request; possibly, the same one you have, too. I simply would like Him to bring me a soul mate with whom I can grow, someone who will love me and not leave me. If not, I would like Him to help me delight in my singleness.

In the Old Testament story of Isaac and Rebekah, you'll find *eight specific steps* to finding a soul mate God's way. The rest is up to Him. His divine wisdom was around a long time before *Glamour*, *Esquire*, or *Cosmopolitan*. He can give you your heart's desire. You've got His Word on it!

❦ 1 ❦

A Hope and a Plan

"Who killed my sister?" sneered the Wicked Witch of the West. "Was it you?"

When Dorothy Gale's house slammed down onto the Wicked Witch of the East, Dorothy found herself feeling quite alone, until Glinda, the good witch, came to her rescue. Sometimes being a single adult is like falling out of the sky into a foreign land. We grew up in homes with parents, siblings, and friends, with lots of conversation, activity, and a feeling of connectedness. Now we're alone, and we want to again belong to someone.

Glinda gave Dorothy the hope that the Wizard could help solve her problems, and the Munchkins gave her the plan: follow the yellow brick road. Along the way, Dorothy enlisted the help of friends who pointed her in the right direction and helped her watch for certain signs. Not unlike dating, Dorothy learned she had to follow the rules to avoid harmful creatures like talking trees and flying monkeys (some of whom I think I dated last year). Finally, before she could approach the Wizard, she had to spend time in preparation at the Emerald City Beauty Salon to become her most beautiful self.

Our story as singles is not so different. To find our soul mate we need to have a plan, get some friends to help, be willing to watch for signs of trouble, endure some nasty creatures, and trust that when things get rough, we'll be lovingly watched and carefully protected. Unfortunately, we don't want to wait, follow rules, or prepare our best. All we want to do is click our heels three times and have everything turn out all right.

Did you know that according to the fast-growing singles web site, *www.eharmony.com*, you are one of between eighty-five and one hundred million singles in America searching for a soul mate? You're certainly not alone!

Today singles search for love in lots of places, some good, some not so good. You may be spending Friday nights at the local grille, signing up with different matchmaking services, or suffering through blind, boring, or belligerent dates. You follow dating rules, breaking the rules, and making up the rules as you go along, usually with heartbreaking results. Some of you try hiding the fact that you're on a frantic mission. Others retreat nobly into work, school, church, or even parenting to hide from the pain of loneliness. You may take various paths to uncover that special someone, but you and I are on the same journey . . . to find love.

Some people have happily settled into their singleness, yet they are still searching. In a turbulent world with deep-felt social issues, is desiring a soul mate something frivolous, shallow, needy, or even desperate? Not at all!

God wired us for love; I don't think He intends for us to go through life without giving or receiving it. The love we experience in our individual lives is meant to grow and reach bigger circles of influence. I believe God has always wanted to help us find love, but we've been trying to do it all by ourselves.

If you ask a dozen people to define what a soul mate is, you'll get a dozen different definitions. Most likely all will agree that a soul mate is a person who knows you, understands you, and shares with you many levels of intimacy (which perhaps no one else can share). A soul mate connects with you mentally, emotionally, and spiritually, hence the word "soul." While you long for such a close connection, are your expectations for such intimacy too high? Does the term soul mate set you up for relationship failure? Maybe, but I think if you read through this book you'll begin to understand, as I have, that marvelous possibilities await you.

Does finding a soul mate really still happen? Absolutely. Will it happen to you? I don't know, but I have hope that great love awaits every single person. And I wrote this book to give you hope.

Planning for Love

Searching for your dream mate doesn't have to be a nightmare, but it can be if you don't have a plan. Many don't plan for anything romantic and feel it will just happen. Young singles hope "Someday my prince will come." Even older singles still cling to the childish fantasy that one day their true love will float down from the heavens. But dreams need to have a practical side. Today's singles would just as soon skip the steps—skip the preparation—skip the work. I can almost hear them thinking: *Just give me the final product. I like the illusion.*

The major reason there are so many failed relationships, broken hearts, divorces, and pregnancies outside marriage today is that people don't wisely or carefully plan. Choices are made based on fantasies, falsehoods, and fairy tales. And, like spoiled little children, people want it easy, and they want it now. Today's society doesn't want to follow the yellow brick road. They don't want others telling them what to do and where to go. They want the feel-good of life, but not the hard-work part. So, some of us wish and wait and foolishly hope our romances will last. Whether we are nineteen or fifty-nine, our hearts get broken, or maybe hardened, and then we start that sickening cycle all over again.

Think about it. For everything important in life, you have a plan, either in your head or on paper. Plans get you where you want to go. You start a savings account, fill out questionnaires, and plan for just the right college. You follow maps to get to your vacation spot, and you plan for retirement. You plan a ski trip to the mountains; you make lists of what you'll need to bring to the party. Your new diet plan will help you reach your goal of losing weight this year. Plans. Lists. Schedules. Steps. So why not have a plan to find your soul mate? It may not be romantic, but it works.

Men and Directions

Asking for directions is part of a good plan. I hate all those stupid jokes about men and directions. I used to laugh, especially at the one about why Moses wandered in the desert for forty years (like all men, silly, he didn't want to ask for directions). But I don't anymore. Girls, for centuries we, too, have failed to ask for directions. Women have refused to ask directions for the right way to live, to love, and to find our soul mates. Women as well as men sleepwalk through life— going to school or work, watching TV at night, shopping on weekends, and doing the same things year after year— wondering why nothing changes and why we're not happy. Both men and women refuse to read books, listen to tapes, take classes, and "ask for directions" about the inner life— the spiritual side of us that will remain when everything else is gone. We never let go, open up, or fully surrender.

In the past few years, though, the media has reported society's increased sensitivity to, and search for the spiritual.

Apparently we have begun to admit that we need God in our lives, yet we still don't ask Him for directions because we want to do it our own way. Many of us have bought into the postmodernist philosophy that our inner voices will tell us what to do and how to do it, so we don't need to ask God or anyone. Consulting our inner voices sounds deeply spiritual, but more often than not the voice we hear is nothing more than our own greedy, scared, hungry, self-centered emotions. Like Dorothy Gale of Kansas, we need two things: real heavenly-based spiritual direction and community support. We can't do it alone.

Faith Versus Fear

Okay, so you agree with the need for a practical plan, but you still have concerns. Will it work? Will I find my true love? Will I be successful? What if I get hurt (again)? Will it be hard? Will it take a long time? So many fears! Let's take it one step at a time. First, we'll define soul mate as offered by different sources, including singles who responded to the soul-mate survey. Then, through the rest of this book, we'll follow the story of Isaac and Rebekah and discover *eight steps* to take in our journey to find true love.

Fears about relationships, or the lack of a having a relationship, are normal. When I'm troubled, one of the easiest and most profound spiritual practices I use is to quickly identify my underlying emotional *fear* and contrast it with *faith*. Sometimes I'm afraid of being alone too long, of having to work too hard, of not having fun, of not being loved. Inwardly, I laugh at the way I think, because if I boiled down every thought, each would begin with: *I want* (companionship), *I want* (security), *I want* (love). Even when I want things that seem good, fear of not getting what "I want" can make me crabby, angry, or depressed, and can even keep me addicted to the bed, the bakery, or the mall.

The fear of not finding a soul mate (or of being hurt in the process) is not cowardly, weak, or wimpy. It's normal. What is weak and wimpy is to deny the fear, ignore it, give in to it, and wish it would go away. Real courage stops, looks fear right in the face, and counters it with faith. Courage surrenders to truth.

The word "courage" in English has the same root as the French *coeur*, which means "heart." In Dorothy's journey to get to the Emerald City, she had three companions, who I think represented parts of her heart or soul—her inner and authentic self. The Scarecrow (her intellect) counseled her with the logical details and information necessary for the trip. The Tin Man (her heart) helped her with the emotional need for, the openness to, and the deep desire for love. And of course, the Cowardly Lion (her will) assisted her as she encountered the facts, the feelings, and the fears, but bravely chose *faith* over *fear*. Remember the frightened feline friend in the enchanted forest when things seemed bleakest? Overwhelmed by fear, he quaked and quivered and wrung his furry tail, but bravely countered his *fear* with *faith*, repeating, "I *do* believe, I *do* believe, I do, I do, I do!"

The lion's belief got him out of the woods, and your faith can too. God can bless you, show you the way, and send you help, even in finding a soul mate.

What Does My Fear Say?

Will I really find a soul mate? What if I don't know where or how to look for love? What if it doesn't work for me? What if my plan fails?

What Does My Faith Say?

God knows exactly what I need and where I need to go to get it. He promises to guide me along the way; I simply must remember to ask for directions!

What Should I Remember?

- *God wants to help me give and receive love.*
- *If I fail to plan, I plan to fail.*
- *Big fears can be overcome by little expressions of faith.*

❧ 2 ❧

Send Me a Soul Mate!

*M*y stepson, Mike, and my nephew, Joe, both teenagers with bleach-tipped hair and baggy pants, were sprawled across the living room sofa talking with me about sex. For years they'd been listening to locker room logistics on sexual activity, but naturally they wanted to know more. I slipped Pam Stenzel's video, *Sex, Love and Relationships*[1] into the VCR and the boys watched intently, shocked at the epidemic rates of sexually transmitted diseases and other physical, mental, emotional, and spiritual consequences of sex outside marriage. After the video, they couldn't quit asking me questions: How can you get a girl to like you? How can you tell if a girl really loves you? What if you catch a disease? How can you make sure a girl is telling you the truth? What if she lies about her past? If she loved me, would she lie to me? How will you know if she's "the one"?

14

"I'm never having sex!" Joe said and then laughed. He looked worried as he thought about what that might mean.

"Well, Joe, if you want to do it right, do it God's way. He's the one who created sex and relationships; He should know how they work best," I told my nephew.

Mike looked serious for a moment and then asked, "Does God tell us how to find our soul mate?"

I was surprised and deeply touched at his sincerity. When Mike was an adorable two-year-old, he saw his mother and dad divorce and watched again in sorrow when my marriage to his father failed. At that moment, I was grateful that my ex-husband made sure that over the years Mike and I could continue our loving relationship of stepmother and stepson. Here he was, feeling safe and sitting on my sofa, pouring out his hopes and fears, and asking about soul mates. Like so many of his generation, he's never been in a home where parents stayed together "in good times and in bad." In spite of it, and perhaps because of it, Mike still longs for one true love, but he hasn't a clue how to find it.

*M*ike Is Not Alone

Singles everywhere, especially young men (like Mike) and young women in their late teens and early twenties, are searching for soul mates. The term soul mate has cropped

up on popular television shows, newspapers, and magazines. A survey from Rutgers University's National
Marriage Project[2] reported that seeking a compatible mate
who shares similar values is not new, but what is new and
surprising is that the soul mate ideal has become the most
desired marital characteristic for this age group—surpass-
ing religion, economics, and even the ability to be a good
mother or father.

What is a soul mate? That's like asking a room full of
men what was the best automobile ever made. The
answers will vary from make to model, but all the cars will
be high maintenance, high performance, and feel as if they
were made just for their driver.

Currently there is no universally accepted definition, and
people continue to argue about whether soul mates are born
or made. When I asked singles to describe a soul mate, most
of the answers supported a deep inner longing for a sense
of perfect union. Despite their ages, their replies show hope,
idealism, and some, even childlike naiveté. Most people
referred to something spiritual, and many listed specific
traits that obviously were missing in their prior relationships. Here are some of the answers I received.

"Someone with the same view of life and who grows with
you. Someone that God has planned for you, hence soul
Mate."—*Frances, age forty-one, single mom recently
divorced*

"A person who God creates for you, who is compatible with you in every way. This doesn't mean they are the same as you, rather . . . they help you, and you help them, fulfill your roles in life, and they help you grow."—*Rachel, married*

"A lifelong companion with whom you could share personal and spiritual things. Because the word soul mate is not gender specific, this person could be male or female and the relationship would be one of emotional and spiritual support."—*Nicki, forty-six, divorced and single for seven years*

"Soul mates put each other first in everything."—*Fred, twenty-eight and single*

"My soul mate will be someone who *wants* to be with me. I'll be a priority in his life. We will share things in common; spiritually, emotionally, and physically. I don't feel that soul mates are made over time; you would know if they are in a matter of months.—*Gina, forty-five, divorced and single for fourteen years*

"A soul mate is born just for you and you have to find them."—*Kathy, sixteen*

"A soul mate is someone who would never lie to you, and you can trust them all the time about everything."—*Miguel, fifteen*

"My soul mate would understand me and appreciate me."—*Charlotte, sixty plus, divorced*

"Someone that you connect with spiritually. Anyone can become a soul mate over time, provided you both want to be soul mates together."—*Dawn, forty-two, married*

"Someone with whom you have an inexplicable connection from early in the relationship and who somehow completely understands you, even when you don't understand yourself, and loves you for who you are anyway."—*Patrick, thirty-three, single*

"Not sure there is such a thing."—*Shelley, thirty-seven, divorced, single three years*

Oprah Winfrey shares some of the characteristics of a soul mate in the December, 2001 issue of O, *the Oprah Magazine.* She writes, "We knew even before September 11 that the very definition of family—connection, trust, support, unconditional love—is what we yearn for and need to feel complete. Everybody needs somebody to count on, no matter what."[3]

I particularly like this definition from Thomas Moore's book, *Soul Mates*:

"A soul mate is someone to whom we feel profoundly connected, as though the communicating and communing that take place between us were not the product of intentional efforts, but rather a divine grace. . . . We may find a soul partner in many different forms of relationship—in friendship, marriage, work, play and family. It is a rare form of intimacy, but it is not limited to one person or to one form."[4]

Fear of being left alone in a tragedy has intensified our search for a soul mate, and fear of a failed marriage has caused us to seek unrealistic perfection in that person. According to recent reports, singles in their twenties want to be with someone who shares their innermost thoughts and feelings, rather than someone rich or of the same religious faith, but they don't necessarily want to marry. The fear of divorcing, like their parents did, may explain the high percentage of young people who live together without the benefits of marriage. Why should we be surprised when they choose to avoid the whole sticky mess of broken vows, failed traditions, and fighting parents? My twenty-six year old niece, Alethea, recently met a young man with whom she hoped to have a relationship. She was discouraged to hear Matt say, "Marriage is the worst business arrangement there is. You go through hell, and then they take half your money. No thanks!" Those who share this sentiment want to live together to avoid divorce. Sadly, those who cohabit have an even higher rate of failed marriages when they do wed. It's a no-win situation.

Young singles aren't the only ones living together to avoid what they see as the pain and failure of marriage. Middle-aged and older divorcees are also avoiding marriage for fear of more failure, heartache, or financial loss. It seems everyone is trying to avoid some kind of pain, but in non-committal relationships they are unknowingly creating whole new heaps of heartache for themselves and others.

Ted and Tiffany

Ted, who's fifty-two, was married twenty-four years with three grown children. He has been divorced for four years, and is experiencing the dating dilemma again. Ted's ex-wife wiped him out financially, taking the kids, the cars, and the house. Although Ted's in the most financially productive years of his life, he hands over nearly 70 percent of his income to his ex-wife for spousal support, since she stayed home all those years and raised the children. Ted is lonely and wants someone to love, but he has fallen back on his high school dating routine: sleep with her first and wait to see if he feels any love later . . . then maybe he'll do the right thing.

Ted's having a typical midlife crisis. Never having developed his inner life, he has reverted back to his youth to recapture that old hormonal high. He dates Tiffany, a twenty-seven-year-old blonde paralegal with a bright mind and a sweet smile. He buys her presents and pays some of her bills, because he feels good in his role as provider. Tiffany loves the security and hopes for children and marriage, but Ted's already raised his children and doesn't want any more. Tiffany hopes to keep Ted sexually involved, thinking he will change his mind. Ted hopes to keep Tiffany emotionally involved so she will change hers. The one with the more assertive personality will finally push the other. They'll start the cycle of arguments and withdrawal and, sooner or later, they'll break up. After some period of grieving, Ted and Tiffany are likely to start looking again for that special someone. If they are like most people, they won't stop and take the time to figure out where they went wrong; they won't learn from their mistakes or devise a new plan for dating. They'll rationalize that things did not work because the other was not their soul mate. Ted, still stuck in emotional and spiritual adolescence, will probably continue to date younger women. Tiffany, stuck looking for that ideal parent, will search for someone to take care of her.

Most of the single women Ted's age are either widows or divorcees—too old for Ted or men like him. Recently, "Still Looking in Colorado" wrote to Ann Landers, "I am a forty-five-year old female . . . divorced for seven years and haven't been in a relationship since. The men my age are looking for women who are in their twenties, are a size five, and have no children."[5]

If these women can find available younger men, the guys are usually ready for children, but now the women are too old for that. Forty to fifty-year-old women could date available older single men in their sixties and seventies, but many women would see that as too old. Still healthy and vibrant, most middle-aged single females are looking forward to a long active life with someone to keep up with them. They don't want to become caretakers to elderly husbands in ten to fifteen years. The oldest single men and women are depressed because their youth and much of their outer beauty is long gone, and no one of *any* age wants them.

All these people are lonely, and all of them want only to love and to be loved. But they continue to follow the same old patterns, making choices that have never worked for them. How do they feel? Headlines in the June 2001 issue of the *Washington Times* reported, "Singles Desperate to Avoid Divorce, Find 'Soul Mate'."[6]

On the West Coast, one Sunday *Los Angeles Times* headline pronounced, "To be single and dating today is to know true despair. Why does relating to the opposite sex seem so impossible?"[7]

In the same article, Jeff Wise, Founder of the American Dating Association, admits, "We think we have the tools for everything and can figure anything out. But the more intelligent and well-educated we are, the more befuddled we are."

A friend shared this quote with me: "Nothing changes if nothing changes." It's pretty obvious that what everyone is doing all by themselves is *not working*!

What We're Forgetting

"Mike," I said to my stepson, "I never thought I'd hear myself say this, but despite our age difference, you and I are facing the same problem. We both want to find someone who will love us forever and never leave us. We're both single and worried. I'm committed this time to doing it right, and, yes, God *does* tell us exactly how to find our soul mate. I'm sure of it!"

Hoping to back up my claim and confident that I would find an answer, I went to the Old Testament. After all, God had found the first soul mate for Adam. I began to read, expecting something to jump out at me, and it did.

Abraham was now old and well advanced in years, and the LORD had blessed him in every way. He said to the chief servant in his household, the one in charge of all the he had, "Put your hand under my thigh. I want you to swear by the LORD, the God of heaven and the God of earth, that you will not get a wife for my son from the daughters of the Canaanites, among whom I am living, but will go to my country and my own relatives and get a wife for my son Isaac." (Gen. 24:1–4)

There it was! A beautiful story of a father's love, a servant's mission, and a son's hope to find just the right spouse. In the first book of ancient Scripture, with the story of Isaac and Rebekah, I found the answer to Mike's question.

Yes, Mike, God does tell us *precisely* how to find a soul mate. Read on.

What Does My Fear Say?

What if no one wants me? Everything I have tried doesn't work. I'm afraid that everything I do will fail. Sometimes I think I might as well forget it.

What Does My Faith Say?

I believe that God can show me exactly how to find a soul mate the right way, but I might have to give up my old ways. I'm ready and willing to do something different. I really am!

What Should I Remember?

- *God created relationships, so He knows how they work best.*
- *I don't have to despair, because love is out there for me.*
- *I am not alone!*

❧ 3 ❧

The Eight Steps

ome with me to a time and place long ago and listen to the story of a father's love for his son, a servant's love for his master, and how two soul mates found each other.

Isaac and Rebekah— An Ancient Love Story

Abraham was the leader of many desert dwelling people, and God had richly blessed him and his wife Sarah with possessions, flocks, herds, and many servants, but no son of their own. Years passed, and when Sarah was old and well past her childbearing years, God miraculously blessed them with a baby boy. The birth of little Isaac brought immeasurable joy to the aged couple, and their son grew to manhood in wisdom and strength.

When Isaac was nearing his forties, Sarah died. While father and son remained in mourning, Abraham began to realize it was time for his son to start a family of his own. In those days, it was customary for the father to arrange the marriages of his children. Finding a wife for Isaac now weighed heavily on Abraham's mind. He called his chief servant, Eliezer, to come before him and swear to carry out the task of finding a suitable spouse for Isaac. After praying to God for direction, Abraham instructed Eliezer exactly where to go to find a bride, and assured him that God promised to send an angel before him to help him on his journey. Eliezer obeyed immediately. Recruiting the best servants to travel with him, he loaded ten strong camels with supplies as well as costly gifts and offerings for the bride and her family.

Abraham had made it clear that the girl should not be selected from any foreign people, but from their own family kinsmen. God had shared with Abraham great plans and promises for his descendants, and the future mother of these many nations would have to be carefully chosen. Eliezer knew that this probably was the most important task his master would ever give him. He worried that once he got to the town he would have no idea how to find Abraham's kinsmen, much less the perfect girl for Isaac. How would he know who she was; could he trust his own judgment? Just before arriving at his destination, Eliezer fell to his knees and begged God for success in his mission and a sign to help him find the girl who could become Isaac's soul mate.

The sign that Eliezer suggested would leave no room for doubt. He would ask for a drink of water from the well, and the girl who not only agreed to give him water, but also offered to water every one of his ten thirsty camels, would be the one. Imagine the huge task that would be for anyone, much less a young girl. It was preposterous to expect anyone to freely offer to spend so much time tending to some stranger's hot, cranky camels. But that's exactly what happened.

Eliezer first spotted Rebekah because she was beautiful. As she approached the well, he noticed that she was not married and was a virgin. So far, so good. Then he quietly watched her as she filled her water jar, noticing how she behaved with others and how she carried herself. She looked good, but would she answer him with the words he longed to hear? Everything had to be just right.

Eliezer hurried to her and asked for a drink. Imagine his surprise and delight when she smiled sweetly, poured him some water, and then offered to water all his camels. Even though his heart must have been racing, he patiently continued to observe her at work. She was a vision to behold and had responded with all the right words, but did she fulfill the mandatory requirement? Was she from Abraham's kinsmen? Eliezer pulled out a gold nose ring and two bracelets and put them on her. Then he asked about her family and if there might be room in their home for him to spend the night. When Rebekah told him who her father and grandfather were, Eliezer realized that she was his master's great niece—she was kin! I'm sure Eliezer couldn't contain his joy, and Scripture tells us he bowed down right then and there to thank and worship God for making his journey so successful.

Eliezer went with Rebekah and told his amazing story to her family around the dinner table that night. Although they were happy for her good fortune, Rebekah's family didn't want to lose her right away. But the young girl was eager to go. She was delighted, as are most young women, at the thought of becoming the bride of a godly man. Rebekah and her nurse left with Eliezer and his men and traveled back to the land of Canaan. As they neared the end of the journey, the party came upon Isaac who was meditating in a field. Their eyes met . . . and the rest is, as they say, history.

Isaac brought her into the tent of his mother Sarah, and he married Rebekah. So she became his wife, and he loved her; and Isaac was comforted after his mother's death. (Genesis 24:67)

* * *

Ah-h-h, a happy ending. In the first part of this love story, we find a faithful manservant being dispatched on a journey to a faraway country to find a bride for his master's son. Not just any bride, but someone unique, someone chosen especially for his son. Wouldn't you like to have a servant bring *you* the mate of your dreams? Do you want God to show *you* a sign? Are you looking for a mate who has saved the best for last and has precious presents to give *you*?

If you are looking for that special someone and want God's blessing in your quest, this book will help you follow the same Eight Steps that Eliezer took to find Isaac his perfect mate.

Step 1: Pray for God's Blessing

Thousands of years ago, Abraham and Eliezer asked for God's blessings . . . and got them. But what about modern times? Is God still available to help? Today we drive Camaros instead of camels and wear Reeboks instead of robes, but some things never change: our need for love, and God's infinite ability to answer our prayers.

Step 2: Seek the Help of Others

Asking others to help is not a sign of weakness—it's smart. In fact, we expect our closest friends to know what we like and get it for us when they see it. We know that the more trusted friends we have helping us, the better our chances are of finding exactly what we want.

Step 3: Prepare Our Best Gifts

When we're getting ready for the big date, we plan ahead by getting the car ready, selecting our best outfit, dropping that extra pound or two, getting our nails done, or making reservations, but have we prepared our best gifts for a lifelong relationship?

Step 4: Look for Things That Matter

He has to be tall, dark, and handsome . . . but will he stand up to his mother for us, get an extra job when money is tight, or stay faithful on a business trip? Too many relationships fail because we don't really know what we want or how to look for it.

Step 5: Ask God for a Sign

Signs and wonders are still possible today, and God is still able to lead us to the desires of our heart. With supernatural and natural signs to point the way, God can help us find a lifetime love, but we must look and listen.

Step 6: Be Willing to Wait

Time is a gift that helps us prepare ourselves for love and allows us to clearly see the other person's heart. Do we want to rush into a relationship that might break our heart, or are we willing to wait for True Love?

Step 7: L.O.V.E. Each Other

While we're getting to know each other, we can L.O.V.E. one another by Listening, Observing, Verifying, and Expressing our needs and wishes. These four simple steps can prevent us from tripping up in the selection process.

Step 8: Save Your Best for Last

Only a fool would entrust his favorite possessions to someone who didn't care, or her heart to a stranger. Most of us have been giving away too much too soon—crying bitterly when it is thrown back at us. We must learn how to save our best for last.

* * *

In beginning this book, you've taken an important step in the long journey of searching for a soul mate. The next eight steps can help you get closer than ever to finding the one true love you seek. Are you ready?

What Does My Fear Say?

Maybe this is just superstition. What if I try it God's way and it fails—then what?

What Does My Faith Say?

Well, my ways haven't been very successful. I believe in God, and I believe His promises to bless me and show me the way to finding love in my life. I'm ready for the first step. Let's go.

What Should I Remember?

- *God wants to bless me.*
- *God wants to lead the way.*
- *God wants to show me signs.*

4

Step 1:
Pray for God's Blessing

hen he prayed, "Oh LORD, God of my master Abraham, give me success today, and show kindness to my master Abraham." (Genesis 24:12)

"Hurry up, Joe! Dad's leaving right now!"

I sighed impatiently and stood over my nineteen-year-old brother, Joe, as he gulped down coffee and ate his raisin toast. It was 1975 and our dad was taking both of us car shopping. This would be Joe's first car and my second. I'd totaled my first car (a yellow Ford Mustang Grande) one weekend on my way home from San Francisco. Joe and I could scarcely contain our excitement during the long drive from Palm Springs to Cal Worthington's dealership in Long Beach. The salesman strolled with us through the huge inventory as the Southern California sunshine glistened off the rows and rows of shiny new and used automobiles of every color. Color was, of course, the most important requisite on my list. I depended on Dad to understand all that mechanical stuff. I wanted blue, so the salesman made a deal for two slightly used Ford Mavericks—mine was a beautiful blue and Joe's was cherry red with a slick racing stripe. We were stylin'!

Dad co-signed the papers for us, set us up with bank financing of $50 monthly payments, and told us he'd see us at home. Joe and I jumped in our cars and pushed the speed limit down Interstate 10 for two hours straight, racing side by side, and cranking up our radios as loud as we could, singing Creedence Clearwater songs at the top of our lungs. When we arrived back in the desert, we got out to admire our new cars and both smelled something burning. "Rose, it's coming from your car!" Joe said. I quickly discovered that I'd been racing home with my parking brake on. Ouch.

In the years following, I always had a husband to buy my car, so it wasn't until I was divorced a few years ago that I had to face what I considered was a difficult task: to buy a car all by myself. I was still hurt and angry that I was alone and forced to shop for a vehicle without my husband's help. I never have understood cars very well, and I just wanted it over with. I didn't want it to be hard or to have to spend much time on research. Why couldn't I just go pick one I liked, sign the papers, and drive it home? Like a lot of people, I went in unarmed and unprepared, hoping that no one would take advantage of me. I'm not blonde, but I sure was dumb.

I paid cash for the worst used car I've ever driven, but it was such a *pretty* color of jade green! The day after I bought it, the entire dashboard split open. I unsuccessfully argued for the dealer to replace it; then I demanded he at least give me a dash mat to cover it up. Over the next year, my troubles included a loud ticking in the dash and a lurching in the engine. A few times the car shook violently and I was overcome by the smell of gas. Little did I know that raw fuel was spilling into my engine, and I could have blown myself up! At first, I resigned myself nobly to living almost martyr-like with my poor purchase. I tried to suffer through it, just thankful that I had a car at all. But after monthly trips to a mechanic, and more talk about ball joints than I care to recall, I was finally advised to spend $2,000 for a new transmission. That was it, no more. It was time for me to resign from my martyrdom.

* * *

I knew I needed to get smart and try a new approach. So I followed Abraham's servant's two-part plan: I sought spiritual leading and then took practical steps to pursue my goal.

I asked God to please give me wisdom, because I was alone now and needed all the help I could get. I remembered taking my Dad car shopping years ago, and now I would take my heavenly Father. I got on the computer and researched for several days. I asked some men that I know what they would buy. I also budgeted in the anticipated costs, and prepared to pay an outrageous interest rate, because my credit had been ruined in the divorce. Then I set out for Toyota of the Desert, asking one more time for a blessing. I prayed that God would bring me a trustworthy salesman (yes, they do exist) and help me to stay open to spiritual leading.

Some people think that asking God to help them with a car is trivial, superstitious, and silly. This usually is based on their observance of, and disgust with, those who see God as a magician. You've heard it: "Send in your contribution and God will make you rich," and maybe drop a Lexus in your lap, too.

Rather than praying for material possessions, I asked God for the gift of wisdom and an openness to His leading. As Bruce Wilkinson shares in his book, *The Prayer of Jabez*, Jabez had a "radical trust" in God's general good intentions toward His people. When Jabez asked for God's blessing, Wilkinson recounts, "He left it entirely up to God to decide what the blessings would be and where, when, and how Jabez would receive them."[1] I've learned that the God I know wants to help me in small things and big, but I must be willing and open to Him to reveal those things to me as I go along.

So as I drove to the dealership, I let God know my general need and asked for his blessings of wisdom and openness. Whenever I do that, I can receive as His blessing:

- a deeper trust in Him and less reliance on my ego
- the courage to overcome fears, even small ones, that keep me in emotional bondage
- an increased wisdom to see and hear truth, whether it is a deep spiritual truth or a little truth in daily details
- a release of my grip on things I want
- patience to let life unfold at a different pace than I expect
- peace that surpasses all understanding
- a greater capacity to know, receive, and give true love to others

How did God answer that day? The manager who normally sits hidden away in the back of the Toyota dealership happened to be walking through the showroom and saw me. It was Dan, my brother Joe's long-time friend, whom I had not seen in years. I had no idea he even worked there! Dan whisked me away into a special office, made me a deal I couldn't refuse at a miraculously low interest rate, and I drove home in a new Toyota Solara that has been the best car I've driven in years.

Can you see the principle that applies to your soul mate search? When I tried to do things without my Father's help or blessing, I made a mess. I didn't want it to be hard; I didn't want to spend the time preparing or educating myself; I didn't focus on what mattered; and I based my choice heavily on outward beauty. I didn't ask for help. I let my fears and the "I wants" stand in the way of responding more maturely to life.

As soon as I drove the green "lemon" home, things started to go wrong. I'd used dashboard mats to cover up problems. I hated paying for the high-priced repairs, but in my stubborn self-reliance, I ended up paying much more for the car than I ever expected. I never felt secure. I imagined breaking down on the highway and getting robbed, dumped, and left for dead. With raw fuel pouring onto the spark plugs, I put myself in real danger a number of times, as well as all those who were around me.

We do the same with relationships. We want it to be easy. We hope that the right one will come along apart from any research, planning, assistance, or discernment. We base our choices on looks, personality, charm, money, or sex—the "color" of the car, but not the character. Because we want the goodies so badly, and we don't want to see any problems, we refuse to look under the engine! Then when things go wrong, we try to live with it, cover it up, make bigger messes, or emotionally endanger others and ourselves.

In my twenties, I asked my earthly father for help. Now I ask my heavenly Father for help and joyfully, life is much better than when I did it on my own. Parents are usually loving providers and protectors who want to help their children. God is the all-loving parent who wants the best for His children—in big things and small—from Solaras to soul mates.

Eliezer Asks for Blessings and Favor

Asking for God's blessings and favor is nothing new. Humans have sought help from God since the beginning of time, recognizing the need for a divine guidance outside themselves. Abraham's servant, Eliezer, knew that. Finding a suitable spouse for his master's son would be no easy task. To insure the success of his search, he partnered with the greatest power known—the Lord God.

Eliezer was seventy years old when he undertook his matchmaking assignment. He'd been with Abraham since he was a young man. In fact, before Isaac was born, Abraham was without an heir, and he thought he would be leaving all his wealth and possessions to Eliezer, his beloved servant. Eliezer, who had started with menial tasks such as tending flocks, rose in stature as the keeper of accounts and had finally become chief over all of Abraham's properties and wealth. More a family member and friend than servant, Eliezer now oversaw the loading of ten camels with precious presents and treasures with which to procure Isaac's soul mate. But it was to be a long journey to the place called Haran and, before their small party left, he expressed his fears to Abraham:

"What if the woman is unwilling to follow me to this land? Should I then take your son back to the land from which you migrated?" he asked.

Eliezer wanted to know what do under all circumstances. What if thieves attacked them on the way? What if he could not find the right woman? What if she refused to come? Then what? He could not give up easily, since he was completely devoted to his master's wishes. Undoubtedly, Eliezer drew upon his faith to conquer his fears.

Eliezer's faith had grown strong over the years. Earlier in Genesis the chief servant had witnessed God's repeated favor and blessings on Abraham. From the time Eliezer was a young man, he saw God promise and then deliver:

- guidance in their travels to foreign lands
- safety for Abraham and Sarah from Pharaoh in Egypt
- an increase in wealth and territory of the family
- protection for Abraham and his people from enemy attack
- direction and protection while they rescued their loved ones
- a long-desired heir (Isaac) to Abraham and Sarah
- a blessing on Abraham's entire family
- signs when Abraham needed or asked for them
- special messengers and guides to help them

Eliezer, whose name means "God helps," didn't know exactly who, how, or when, but he was willing to pray for help, was open to spiritual leading, and would take the necessary steps to find a soul mate for Isaac. Eliezer knew that God had acted favorably time and time again, and now, he trusted that God would lead him, send help, show him signs, and continue to let it turn out favorably.

In contrast to Eliezer, we often fail to ask for God's blessings because we don't fully believe. Or we get so distracted that we don't even consider praying. Perhaps living life on our own has gone okay, maybe for years, so we've been fooled into thinking we can handle it all by ourselves.

The Miracle Worker

Consider the story of Helen Keller, the little girl made blind and deaf by a mysterious disease when she was only nineteen months old. The book, *The Miracle Worker*, is beautifully written; the movie version is poignant and profound. Out of pity, Helen's parents overindulged her in some areas and neglected her in others. She was an angry, frustrated, and out-of-control child, who manipulated, withdrew, and threw marvelous tantrums. Although she was bright and intelligent, her parents could not give Helen what she really needed. Finally, her fed-up parents hired a teacher, Annie, to come and work with Helen.

The teacher did something that surprised everyone. She insisted on taking the girl away to a nearby cottage so the two of them could live alone. No loving mom, no doting dad, and no outside distractions. Annie knew that in order to be able to give her gifts to the child, Helen would have to trust her. To trust her, Helen would first have to *know* her—inside and out.

With her new teacher, Helen used all her tricks to stay in control and get her way. When Annie said yes, Helen was happy. When Annie said no, Helen threw a fit! But Annie patiently waited and continued to love Helen, saying both yes and no to her requests.

The more intimate time she spent with Annie, the more Helen knew her teacher's character and developed authentic trust. Then Annie could share her gifts. Shortly after that, Helen experienced her first real awakening, a moving scene in the book and on the screen. With her hand held closely in Annie's, she learned to sign the word "water." Over the years, Helen's trust for Annie grew to a deep and lasting love. As a result, Helen learned to read, write, and speak. In 1904 she graduated with honors from Radcliffe College.[2]

Our relationship with God is like that. We never really get to know him because we have transferred our worldviews onto Him and we see Him as unsafe, distant, or uncaring. Possibly, because of daily distractions and noise of life, we don't even think about God. When that happens, He can't give us His full favor or blessings. It may be time to move away from the routine or past patterns and spend more time talking to Him, reading about Him, and learning from others about His love for you. While no one can ever fully know God, we can move from childish levels of just knowing *about* Him, to knowing His character so intimately that we begin to trust Him in all things.

From the beginning of time, God has called us to Himself. Our deepest desires for intimacy, love, and belonging—our desire for a soul mate—come from Him, and ultimately they are for Him.

God does not always give you what you want. He *does* give you everything you would want if you could see what He sees and know what He knows. Don't deny your desire for a soul mate, and don't demand that God provide one for you immediately. Instead, share it with your heavenly Father and ask His special blessings. Put your hand in His and let Him teach you new and wonderful things. Pray that He will let it turn out favorably for you. Then stay tuned in to His voice, and expect lots of miracles.

* * *

"[Real prayer] has not been tried and found wanting; it has been found difficult and not tried."—Gilbert K. Chesterton

What Does My Fear Say?

Sometimes I don't believe that God really wants to help me with little things or those items that seem selfish. I worry that I am really alone and have to make decisions by myself. Sometimes I worry that God won't bless me because I don't deserve it.

What Does My Faith Say?

No one deserves God's blessings, but He wants to give them to me anyway. From the beginning of time, God has done whatever it takes to draw me closer to Him. Like a loving father, he wants to bless me, favor me, and help me grow in love.

What Should I Remember?

- *God is like a loving parent who wants only the best for me in all things.*
- *Even though God is like a parent, I should quit acting like a baby!*
- *I need to develop a daily habit of praying to God for all my needs.*

5

Step 2:
Seek the Help of Others

*E*liezer didn't travel alone. On the journey to Haran, he took ten of the strongest camels; costly gifts for the young woman he prayed to find; food, clothing, and water for their assembled group; and enough servants to set up and take down camp each day. He undoubtedly talked about their mission with his fellow travelers and relied on their physical and emotional support along the way. When they arrived outside the city of Nahor, their caravan stopped at the community well. At the end of the day, travelers would gather there under the date palm trees to water their camels and trade stories. In the cool of the evening, the women of the town would come to fill their water jars.

Men and women have changed little since then. I'm guessing that Eliezer and the other men in his party were like guys after work on a Friday night. It had been a long day, they were thirsty, and on the hunt for a good woman (in this case, a wife for Isaac). This was where the action was. Although they shared a serious purpose and were looking for just the right girl, I imagine they laughed and joked and scanned every female face at the busy watering hole.

"Hey, Eliezer! What about her?" one may have asked, with a grin and an eager nod from the others. Maybe Eliezer looked and admired the rounded beauty who had just strolled by.

"Whoo-wee! Check out the blue veil at ten o'clock!" Poor Eliezer. So many women, so little time! I'm sure he appreciated the helpful input from the men, but ultimately he would have to make the final decision. While he valued their advice, he still tested who would be the future bride against that which God would reveal to him. That's what we need in our search for a soul mate: practical, useful help from others and divine guidance. Why? Because this is one of the most important decisions we will ever make; one that will affect every part of our life, for the rest of our life.

Good Help and Bad Help

Whenever I need help with anything, I fight the automatic urge to do it all myself. First, I stop and ask for God's help; then, I drive to my local bookstore. My personal library is the size of a small continent, and my research for this book took me to publications on love, sex, singles, soul mates, dating vs. courtship, 101-ways-to-get-a-man or woman, and, of course, those made-to-be-broken rules. I've read all the top-selling advice, agreed with some, laughed at others, and happily thrown some in the trash. Like advice on any topic, there is the sensible, the outrageous, and what I think is the most dangerous of all: advice that sounds spiritual, uses words like "sacred" and talks about a "loving universe," but is the most misleading of all. You may initially agree with these "new age" goals of maturing mentally, emotionally, and spiritually to a healthy level of self-love and self-acceptance. But you must turn your back on books that teach that you are just like a god, or god is really you. Heaven help us if we place our trust in the narcissistic trinity of me, myself, and I.

One book I read encouraged the reader to summon an inner spirit guide; another said to forget the rules and "make your own d—- rules!" by listening to your heart, soul, and mind. Listening inside yourself is good if you're seeking God's inner voice, but any other voice can be dangerous. Hearts, souls, and minds can be damaged. The heart can be deceiving, the emotions can be out of control, and the world can sway your thinking. Your ego and intellect can be as overblown as the Goodyear Blimp or as underdeveloped as earthworm larvae. Other voices you hear may be your Mom's or Dad's, your teachers', your peers', and even the voices from movies, television, and magazines. While you should use the God-given gifts of your mind, emotions, conscience, and intuition, you must carefully test them against what God has revealed in the past and what He makes known to you today. Want to find your soul mate? Keep in touch with God.

Where Can You Get Help Finding a Soul Mate?

I made two lists. My first list was of places that offer solid, healthy tips in finding love. My second list was of places that offer negative help and could steer me in the wrong direction. Take a look at each list:

Where to Get GOOD Advice/Help	Where to Get BAD Advice/Help
Parents	Parents
Family & Friends	Family & Friends
Books and Tapes	Books and Tapes
Seminars	Seminars
Places of Worship	Places of Worship
Pastors and Counselors	Pastors and Counselors
Dating Services	Dating Services
On-line Singles Sites	On-line Singles Sites

Surprised? Most people have their minds made up about what is good and bad, but I suggest we look for the good and bad in every possible source before we close the door that God may have opened for us.

*P*arents

Young singles probably will laugh at the idea of consulting parents. It's natural for teens to separate from parents and find their own way in life. In this stage, a person's experiences are extending beyond the family. They focus on developing a separate identity and faith. Personal friends (and their social values) seem much more trustworthy. As a result, the advice of friends carries greater weight than does the advice of parents—and that's not always good.

When I questioned a few local teenage girls about asking for their parents' help in finding the right person, their answers ranged from "You gotta be kidding!" to "Yeah, I'd ask them if I knew I'd still have the right to make up my own mind."

Granted, there are parents, no matter their age, who have little wisdom and hand out terrible advice. Some parents have never matured emotionally past their own adolescence and have never developed a depth of inner wisdom. They may be uninterested, uncommunicative, or even abusive. Others have keen insight, but are afraid to speak up. Dr. Neil Clark Warren shares this insight in his book, *Finding the Love of Your Life*, "Some parents lack courage. They are well aware that their child is charging into a relationship that is fraught with danger. But in the name of being 'supportive parents,' they remain positive—and silent! They often feel heavy guilt when the marriage falls apart just as they thought it would."[1] But as a general rule, most parents have attained some wisdom, and normally hand out thoughtful advice.

In today's ever-increasing fatherless society, it's sad to realize that we can't depend on our father's help like Isaac depended on help from Abraham. Ideally, the first person each of us should be able to go to for help is our fathers. Fathers were created to care for their families and help meet their needs, especially in finding a good mate. Throughout history, parents were often the source for selecting their children's prospective husband or wife. As with all human endeavors, however, this practice was never perfect. Some arranged marriages were disasters. But at forty years of age, Isaac trusted and respected his father's ability to find him a suitable mate.

In previous generations, fathers and mothers were a source of wisdom and advice. It has only been in the last few decades that children have stopped asking for their parents' help, and men have stopped asking a father's permission for his daughter's hand in marriage. In the 1960s (when I was a teenager) the predominant slogans of youth were, "God Is Dead," "Hell No, We Won't Go" (to war with Vietnam) and, with the advent of free love, "If It Feels Good, Do It!" In efforts to bring balance and independence to a sometimes, parental-smothering system, the youth culture brought in the attitudes of disobedience, rebellion against authority, and a will to do whatever felt good—no matter what. The youth of the 60s ignored the fact that fathers (and mothers) could be of wise counsel in helping find suitable marriage partners.

With self-will run rampant, many young people chose to ignore a very valuable resource—fathers. I had a dad who was wise, mature, and actively involved in my life. He listened to me when I was a toddler, loved me through good and bad times, and gave me strong, fatherly guidance in many areas. If your dad has been a part of your life and your communication with him is open and loving, then go to him and ask him to help in your search for a soul mate.

If your parents haven't been there for you because of death, divorce, or have been uninvolved for various other reasons, look around for a parent substitute. Do you have a loving stepparent? grandparent? aunt? uncle? older brother? older sister? pastor? rabbi? Maybe you're an older single, divorcee, widow, or your parents have died. Whatever your age or sex, you need strong, loving male or female mentoring. Ask God to show you someone who can help. If no one comes to mind, remember you can always go to your heavenly Father, any place, any time.

Family and Friends

While Mom and Dad may be too close for some, a trusted uncle, aunt, or cousin may be the person God can use to guide you. I have been blessed with thirty nieces and nephews, and most of them are single and in their mid-twenties. Last summer I invited my adult nieces—Alethea, Kristin, Teresa, Sara, Lisa, and Joanna—to a weekend at the beach in San Clemente. We shopped 'til we dropped, pigged out on pizza, and went to Disneyland for the day. At night we stayed up late talking about what else? *Men.* Even though I'm twice as old as some of my nieces, we still want to find a man who would love us and never leave us. Each of my niece's parents have been divorced, and they don't want it to happen to them. They know I have been divorced and now understand a lot of what *not* to do in making life choices. Because they have shared their histories with me and know that I love them (and their parents), I was able to impart some hard-earned wisdom. It was a fun weekend, and we all learned from and supported each other.

But watch out for nosy, controlling, and intrusive relatives who have no idea what they are talking about. Look at their relationships and their lives. Do you respect them and their values? Do they have experience, or was the last time they dated back in the hippie era, when everyone made love not war (and ended up divorced)? Blood does not mean brilliance!

ℬ ooks and Tapes

To obtain my driver's license, I had to read books, watch movies, and listen to lectures. Many jobs require attendance at training sessions and reading educational material. Buying a car (ask me!) necessitates reading the latest reports on car makes, models, and their respective performance. If you purchase a computer, you refer to manuals, reference books, even books for "dummies," folders, files, and other printed material. So . . . why do you think you don't need to investigate the ins-and-outs of dating and courting when selecting the most important human relationship in your life? Good books can help you understand yourself and understand others so that you make a wise choice in life. No matter what your age, every budget (including mine) should have a monthly amount for "continuing education."

Have you ever gone to a restaurant, studied the menu, and selected a high-priced but scrumptious looking meal? You may have savored the steak, relished the ragout, but choked on the cauliflower. Does that mean it was a bad meal? Does it mean that you got nothing out of it? No, you ate what was good and avoided the rest as soon as you recognized or tasted it.

As a youngster, my brother, Joe, hated lima beans. One day after cleaning his plate he asked to be excused. Joe went directly to the bathroom, pulled out his napkin (which was carefully hidden in his pocket), and flushed all his lima beans down the toilet. Likewise, you need to keep your reading tastes in line with what you know is right and good. Don't discard the whole meal (of books, tapes, and advice) because part of it wasn't suitable. Digest what is good—flush the rest.

Seminars

Companies spend billions of dollars every year sending their employees to seminars to keep them on top of the latest information. They know added training will increase the employees' productivity and success. And when it comes to finding a soul mate, seminars can keep you up-to-date on relationship issues. They can serve as mini-vacations when you take along a friend or two. You'll probably make additional new friends who are in the same situation—single and looking for a soul mate. Caution: be as careful about seminars as you would about books, tapes, or other helps. Check them out first, and don't believe everything you hear.

Places of Worship

I hate to say it, but I have met the weirdest and creepiest men at church. Some of the men I interviewed also concur, saying they found the neediest, most troubled women at church. Churches, temples, and other places of worship are filled with human beings who are hurting, lost, and often not ready for a healthy relationship. Be glad they attend, but you need to get rid of the naïve idea that church is always a safe place to find someone.

Almost everyone wants to grow together spiritually, so finding a soul mate who shares a common level of faith should be an absolute "must have" on anyone's list. I won't date a man who is not of the same faith. I've tried it. Because the men were smart, charming, vibrant, and handsome, I almost killed myself trying to make it work. It's like that dress that's the perfect color, style, and price— but it's two sizes too small. Suck it in, stand up straight, and don't move . . . and you will find yourself exhausted, irritated, and ready to bust loose. The "dress" won't be happy either!

Start with church, but keep your eyes and ears open.

Pastors and Counselors

Just like doctors, dentists, and car salesmen, most pastors and counselors are good—some are not. During a recent radio interview for a prior book *Healing the Heartbreak of Divorce*,[2] I told the talk show host that I was writing a book about finding a soul mate. He shared a sad story about his divorce:

"When I met my wife at church, she was attracted to two other young men. I knew I was third choice, but I proposed first. When my wife-to-be went to the pastor's wife for advice, she was asked, 'Do you love Bill?' She responded with an honest no. Then the pastor's wife proceeded to ask, 'Do you respect him?' My wife said yes, so the pastor's wife advised her, 'Well, marry him. The love will come.' Rose, the love never came. We married for all the wrong reasons, and after two years, she made it known that she was attracted to another man. After four years, we started talking divorce, and after twenty years, she announced one day, 'I've been faking it for twenty years. I'm outta here!' Our kids were devastated, as was I. My wife let our sixteen-year-old daughter read her diary, where she wrote that she had never loved me and the reasons why. My daughter turned against me, and I lost my whole family."

So much pain! The church counselor was right that true love does take time to reach its deepest levels after the wedding. But much more than respect needs to be present when people decide to marry. I respect many men, but that doesn't mean those relationships hold all the necessary ingredients for a healthy marriage. Sometimes singles base their decisions on a counselor's advice and following that advice seems like the easiest answer, if one is confused or overwhelmed. Society places professional counselors on a pedestal; they tend to think professionals can't be wrong. When a person takes another's advice too quickly, they may end up like this radio interviewer and his ex-wife. The result: they defrauded each other of a true soul mate relationship, set a sad example for their children, and ended up middle-aged and miserable.

Dating Services

My grade school friend, Tom, and I still keep in touch by e-mail. Although we both started out in first grade together with the same idealistic hopes and dreams, we are now both single again and wading through the shark-infested waters of weekend dates. I told him I was investigating dating services and asked his opinion as a male. He said he thinks people have to be as careful with them as with any way to meet new people—take normal precautions and take your time. But he also shared, "Rose, when I read a woman's profile— her age, how many kids she has, where she works, what she likes to do, her pet peeves, her political outlook, her basic religious beliefs and see her photo—I can get in five minutes what it would take me three dates and probably over $300 to find out. It can save a lot of time and money!"

I laughed, but had to admit it made some sense, from a man's point of view, as well as from a woman's. We girls spend almost as much money on the new outfit that we have to have, the shoes to match (and purse if we go all out!), the hair and nails, the baby-sitter if necessary, and burning off the calories we pack on at the fancy restaurants where first dates usually take us. Word of caution: use your head with dating services. If it seems legitimate and is well referenced, go for it. Never give out your home phone number. Never meet alone in a secluded spot. Don't believe everything you read, check out everything, and take your time. And don't forget to ask God to give you either a sense of peace or convict you to look elsewhere. When in doubt, *don't*.

On-line Singles Sites

Computer technology offers a hot new place for people who are looking for soul mates. No new dress and shoes or expensive dinner is required. You can spend lots of time talking and discovering what you like and don't like. Some people have had success in finding dates and mates on-line; others have not. According to Jupiter Media Metrix, five million U.S. singles have embraced on-line matchmaking as an alternative to set-ups and singles bars.[3] At *www.eharmony.com*, a fast-growing matchmaking site, founder Neil Clark Warren reports, "We have experienced record numbers of users to our site . . . indicating that many singles across the country are seeking long-term, committed relationship."[4] For a generation weaned on e-mail and on-line relating, clearly this soul mate search tool is not going anywhere in the near future.

I signed up with a reputable on-line dating service, completed an extremely lengthy questionnaire (which I liked), and was assured I would be matched only with someone who was as close as possible to my "perfect match." I shared with the dating service the following data about myself:

- Educated, California girl; 5'7" in bare feet, so when I wear high heels, which I love, I am at least 5'8" to 5' 10".
- Most comfortable in jeans and T-shirts, but also love to wear St. John and expensive glitz.
- Communicative and verbally expressive, with a sharp mind (in some areas!) and a love for people.
- Talkative with others, share ideas and opinions, and, if we have dessert and coffee to sustain us, I can chat (and of course, listen to you, too) into the night.
- At peace with and need quiet time, but am outgoing and must party every once in while.
- Independent, but also like to follow a strong man and let him lead.

So, with whom did this dating service match me up? A man who was described as follows:

- Nearing seventy and old enough to be my father.
- 5'4".
- Limited in his English-speaking skills.

- Preferred an easy-going life with quiet evenings at home.
- Hated to socialize (introvert).
- So emotional that he "knew he wore his heart on his sleeve" (needy).
- Loved his dear mother before God (although she was long dead).
- Definitely laid-back and low-key

But he was an engineer and had a lot of money. So? Sigh . . . no, thanks.

* * *

I've read articles that warn about the dangers of finding Mr. or Ms. Right on-line. They say computer contact is not the same as real live interaction. Well, as we say in California, "No, duh!" Of course it's not the same; of course it can be dangerous; yes, we can be stupid; and yes, the other person can lie in his or her e-mail or on the phone. We can be seduced, tricked, or endangered. But let's not push the panic button right away.

Do you realize that many of our great-grandfathers and grandmothers met and courted by mail correspondence? They often married without ever meeting each other first. Sometimes their parents arranged the marriages sight unseen. Settlers in the West would run ads in big city newspapers for a bride, and women would pack up their wagons and come-a-runnin'. In a way, mail-order brides were the predecessors to today's e-mail engagements. Some worked, some didn't, but today's generation isn't the first to have difficulty meeting and finding a soul mate.

If your trusted Uncle Fred set you up with his neighbor's son, even there, lies might be involved. Fred's friend can be as masquerading as the computer creep. Did Uncle Fred pull a financial statement and get three references on this guy? No matter where you meet someone, you have to be careful. No matter who recommends them to you, take time and check them out. It's not a matter of fear, but of wisdom. Yes, God can bless your computer search for a soul mate, but remember:

- Don't give out your real name, address, or phone number.
- Set up a separate screen name just for computer dating.
- Do a thorough search of on-line sites; there are hundreds. Don't settle for the first one.
- Try discovering each other through e-mails—without a photo. Looks can turn you off from a good match, or keep you hooked with a lousy one.
- Always get a photo before you meet.
- Never send money to an e-mail contact.
- Ask a million questions. If they don't want to answer or feel pressured, slow down. If they stay closed, forget it.

- Don't agree to meet alone, ever.
- Don't rush or give too much too soon.
- Use your head. Get a friend's input. Pray for wisdom!

ars

What society calls a bar may be a smoke-filled den of depravity to some, or the wine counter at an upscale steakhouse. Whatever you call it, or wherever it is—a bar is never a good place to find a soul mate. Ask the highway patrol. They know liquor brings danger, misery, and death to people who aren't sober while traveling. Every state in the union has large penalties for drinking and driving. Even beyond the physical dangers, there can be mental, emotional, and spiritual penalties—some that might last a lifetime—when you're not thinking with a clear head. Alcohol *always* impairs judgment, and along with your favorite lipstick, good judgment is the one thing you want with you at all times!

Bars or night clubs are also a hot bed (no pun intended) for one night stands—now called hookups—where two people meet, have casual sex, and have no intent of any future relationship. That couldn't be a bigger lie. While it's easier for a man to isolate the emotional part of himself, a woman's heart is often filled with attachment and hopes, whether she admits it or not. If you want to pick the cream of the crop for your lifelong soul mate, why get emotionally attached some night in an alcohol-induced stupor, where everyone looks good in the dark? It's just plain stupid.

Ways Others Can Help

Honest Feedback—Ask your friends, family, or counselor if they think you're a good catch. A trusted friend, especially one who is mature enough to be honest with you, can be invaluable in helping you work on areas that may be in the way of your finding a soul mate. Are you too anxious? Too controlling, loud, demanding, shy, passive, or dull? Do you need a makeover? Ask your friend to rate you on a scale of one to ten in every area you can think of, and then take steps to change if you think you should. Friends can help you find the right person or become the right person.

Keeping Their Eyes Open—Do others know something about your potential new mate—his/her family and friends—that you don't know or see? When I was nineteen, I was engaged to the man I saw as my ticket out of the house and away from Mom. Everyone but me noticed that his father was controlling and verbally abusive, and that his mother walked around in an almost incoherent state, after having been in and out of mental hospitals for nervous breakdowns. H-m-m-m-m . . . do you think someone should have tried to talk me out of it? I was so naïve, so desperate to get out of the house, maybe I would not have listened. But again, maybe I would have.

Keeping Your Grocery List—In chapter seven (Look for Things That Matter), I'll help you make a specific list of what you want and don't want in a soul mate. Every friend, relative, or coworker that might be helping in your search should have a copy of your "grocery list." You never know who God can use to help bring two people together.

Prayer—Do you believe in the power of prayer? I'm sure that when Eliezer left Canaan for Haran, Abraham watched from outside his tents. As the caravan of swaying camels and clouds of sand grew smaller in the distance, perhaps he uttered a prayer, "Bless them, O Lord, and keep them safe. May it turn out favorably for my servant." You can and should pray for safety and success in this journey for a soul mate.

What Does My Fear Say?

I don't really think anyone can help me. It seems too hard and too much work to read books, to listen to tapes, and to get others' help. Besides, what if my family or friends don't like the person that I like? It's my life; why should I get help?

What Does My Faith Say?

I don't have to be afraid of getting help. God gave me free will, and I don't have to do what others tell me I should do. I just have to be smart enough to listen and to give it some thought. Besides, I can trust that God will help me see what is wise advice and what is not.

What Should I Remember?

- *I'm not so smart I can't benefit from the help of others.*
- *God can use all kinds of people, places, and things to help me find true love.*
- *If I don't seek help, I might miss God's blessing.*

❦ 6 ❦

Step 3:
Prepare Your Best Gifts

Then the servant took ten of his master's camels and left, taking with him all kinds of good things from his master. He set out for Aram Naharaim and made his way to the town of Nahor. (Genesis 24:10)

It was the custom then, and still is today, to present gifts to a potential bride and her family as part of the courtship ritual. Eliezer possibly brought precious oils and ointments, perfumes, candies, spices, homespun fabrics, blankets, jars, jugs and other handcrafted pottery, as well as combs, ribbons, earrings, and bracelets. Gifts for the family might have included tools and weapons for the men, yards of strong ropes and leather, and toys for the children. Nothing would be too extravagant to convince the young maiden to leave her home and become a bride.

We do the same when we lavishly spend our time, money, and energy to woo another. Giving gifts can show sincerity, kindness, and generosity on the part of the giver. But it's the precious inner gifts that endure when the dinners are over and the candy box is empty. When I surveyed people about what they wanted in a soul mate, not one person mentioned oodles of possessions, but they all wanted "gifts" nonetheless: gifts of trust, shared ideals, communication, intimacy, support, leadership, loyalty, and undying love.

Why We Need to Prepare Our Gifts

Like Eliezer, you need to begin your search for a soul mate with a full caravan of inner gifts that will attract someone of the type, quality, and character you seek. If you're lazy, stubborn, or selfish, you'll probably not attract someone who is hard-working, balanced, and mature (unless you're drop-dead gorgeous, but then *that* will never last!). If you're extremely overweight, smoke like a chimney, or have other addictive behaviors, someone who is health-conscious, disciplined, and balanced probably will not want you for a soul mate. Like attracts like. To *find* the right person, you have to *be* the right person.

When the right maiden appeared at the well, Eliezer had to be ready. You and I need to be ready too. How can anybody be the right one for you if you are not ready? Columnist Jan Denise Soroka asks, "If you find the perfect car and you can't pay for it, is it really the perfect car for you? If you wait for the perfect wave, and it comes along before you're skilled enough to handle it, is it still the perfect wave for you? And if you encounter the perfect partner while you're still figuring out who you are, is he or she really perfect for you?"[1]

Before their wedding day, people will try completely new hairstyles, cut off their mustache, change their image, lose weight, or try just about anything new and different to become the very best they can be for the "big day." Even though you don't know your wedding date, this can be a time in your life to bring your personality into better balance, to begin to integrate what has been ignored, to embrace what has been denied, and to become the best you can be. Preparing your inner gifts ahead of time will:

- Sharpen your skills and make you more balanced.
- Spur you to greater levels of maturity.
- Increase your confidence.
- Increase your feelings of contentment with your own life.
- Make you attractive to other people of all ages and both sexes.

- Result in a higher quality of life whether or not you find a mate.
- Increase greatly your chances of finding the love of your life.

*T*ime for a Makeover?

Imagine you've already found your soul mate. You deeply love him or her and want to give this person the very best of everything, all the time. You want to please your soul mate in every area. You desire to look and be your best, even as they do for you. Question: why wait until you have found this special person? Right now you can take some immediate steps by giving yourself an inner and outer make over. If you're like most people, you've already spent a small fortune on beauty products, clothes, or other items to make yourself attractive on the outside. Good for you, but how does your *heart* look? What about looking good "from the inside out"?

Looking inside yourself is one of the hardest things to do and one of the most overlooked areas of education. Dr. Gary Lawrence, author of *Rejection Junkies*, says, "People who study all and remain ignorant of themselves have missed the greatest education of all."[2]

A frequent guest on national television, author and speaker "Dr. Phil" (Phillip C. McGraw, Ph.D.) has written a book that became a number one bestseller on the

New York Times Best-seller List. It's called *Self Matters—Creating Your Life from the Inside Out*. Don't confuse the title of McGraw's book with egotistic self-centeredness. The point of "self matters" is that every person needs to look beyond surface living and look inwardly. Don't be afraid to ask the question, "What part is God playing in the development of my spiritual, inner needs?" Could it be that the current social troubles stem from an over-exaggerated focus on the exterior and a failure to develop the interior—the inner self of spirituality, character, maturity, morality, and beauty?

My friend, Tammy Bennett, author of *Looking Good From the Inside Out*, works monthly with author/speaker, Florence Littauer and me at an advanced mentoring seminar for public speakers, called "Upper CLASS." The seminar guides speakers who want to improve their presentation and platform image. First, we help them improve the quality and content of their spoken messages. Next is our "fun" day. I help them with their colors and clothing style, and Tammy does hair and makeup. It has been exciting for us to see people of all ages and walks of life sit down in our chairs, be willing to learn and change, and even go for the unexpected. Something amazing happens when the student is totally open to growth and new directions. As the seminar students' trust in me grows, I can bring out an external beauty in a way they never imagined. Some have even let me cut their hair! Working together, teacher and pupil can achieve greater creativity, along with higher levels of inner and outer beauty.

God wants to do a similar makeover in every person's life—to bring about the growth and beauty that was dormant before. Like any makeover, we must trust Him—and cooperate with Him—and He will bring out an inner and outer beauty that will both dazzle and delight.

The Eight Areas of Gift Giving

As you read through this chapter, you might want to list some immediate changes you could make in each of the following eight areas of gift giving.

1. *Physical*

Even though it's what's inside the stem that counts, the flower's outer beauty first attracts the bee. Outward appearance includes your style as well as your physical health. It's comprised of your makeup, hair, clothing, and scent, all of which make specific unspoken statements. But outer beauty reflects inner attitudes that can repel or attract the "bee" you want.

Some important questions you need to ask: Are you getting enough exercise to keep fit, energetic, and stay at a healthy weight? Does your body health and image reflect discipline and balance, or lack of such? What would someone assume about your character by looking at the way you care for you body? What messages are you sending about how you value yourself? Do you dress to seduce or sexually ensnare? Do you wear too much makeup, perfume, or cologne? Too much jewelry? Are you modest or immodest?

Don't be satisfied in simply being washed and dressed; and don't let your appearance reflect a glaring lack of awareness about life and the world around you. If you put no thought or effort into how you look or smell, or refuse to have any style sense, you're functioning in the extreme realm of apathy, rebellion, or stubbornness. What unspoken messages does your appearance give? What kind of person (with what values) will your dress attract? Your physical appearance often is the first indicator of your inner balance or maturity.

2. *Financial*

Your attitudes about and the way you handle money can be the number one killer of romance in any relationship. Couples fight over finances more than anything else, although money is only the symptom of deeper, underlying attitudes and expectations. If you want your soul mate to be able to handle money maturely, then give them that same gift. Do you need help in making and staying on a budget? Then get help. You can learn some quick and easy financial skills through books, seminars, or classes. Your soul mate does not deserve to struggle with someone who is fearful of, irresponsible with, or addicted to money. Nor will they be attracted to someone who is.

Do you spend every cent you make? If so, financial worries and anxieties set you up to seek a soul mate who is a rescuer. Eventually, that newly found "rescuer" may come to resent you, and resentment kills intimacy. If you can discipline yourself to live below your current income as a single individual, with money to save each month, you will bring a valuable gift to your soul mate. You'll also sleep better, have better health, and be happier . . . which can work like a magnet in attracting people who are the same!

3. *Intellectual*

The other day a drop-dead gorgeous, hunk of a man in workout clothes walked into my office. My secretary, Kristi, and I immediately shot each other that knowing glance, then waited to see what he wanted. This Adonis had a chiseled face, dark eyes, perfect hair, and big bulging biceps. But the minute he opened his mouth and started talking, Kristi and I exchanged another look—of disappointment. I don't know if the poor guy had a mental disability, had burned himself out on drugs, or what, but he couldn't carry on an intelligent conversation. It almost made us want to cry to hear him jabber, talking in circles that we could barely understand. "What a waste!" Kristi said when he left.

If you've had limited schooling or have not kept yourself educated in other ways, Harvard graduates will not be looking to you as their soul mate. When emotions cool and looks fade, soul mates have to have an intellectual compatibility. Just because you're a good person with a good heart doesn't mean that more highly educated people will look past that wide cavern of intellectual shortcomings. Say it again and memorize it: like attracts like. Not only that, like *sustains* like over time.

Just as you feed your body, you have to consistently feed your mind with intellectual food. Like your body, the mind needs to be stretched beyond its comfort level to increase in strength and beauty. How can you exercise your mind and keep it strong and growing? Question everything. Look past the obvious. Develop a curiosity about life, and read . . . read . . . read!

4. *Emotional*

"Baby" was a roly-poly puppy who shoved his way past all the other pups to get most of his mom's milk. While he grew bigger and fatter, the rest of the pups got skinnier and weaker, and the runt of the litter even died. As Baby got fatter, he also got greedier, and soon he could barely walk! The mother dog should have pushed Baby away and let the other puppies feed, but she either was too tired, sick, distracted, or maybe just lacked good sense. Whatever the reason, she hurt her whole family by indulging one and not caring equally for the others.

God made us as spirit and body, mind and emotions. Each part of us needs to be fed, and if one is out of balance, all parts suffer. Emotions and feelings are part of our whole being. They bring balance to the intellect and enhance our spiritual and physical selves. But they can be like Baby, taking most of our energy and becoming self-indulgent.

Some may learn to handle their emotions, but others stay stuck in emotional imbalance. If you're stuck, you need a "mother" to gently but firmly nudge you back into emotional balance. You might need outside help in handling your emotions, no matter how old you are.

When I was growing up, anyone who went to see a psychologist or psychiatrist was considered desperately whacked out. Yet when my body was sick, Mom took me to the doctor. When I had a cavity, she took me to the dentist. When I needed music lessons, she took me to the piano teacher, and when I needed to learn algebra, she sent me to school. My folks didn't mind paying paid good money for those services. They considered it an investment not an expense.

I'm glad that today, when I need help learning about or handling my emotions, I am willing to go to a therapist, psychologist, psychiatrist, family counselor, or pastor who can help me grow and develop that beautiful part of me called emotions.

If you are emotionally troubled, you will attract people at the same level of emotional maturity. Healthy people are attracted to healthy people. To stay strong, fit, and emotionally healthy, you might even consider visiting a trusted, professional counselor for an annual checkup.

5. Personal

Do you know who you are? Are you in touch with what excites and satisfies you mentally, emotionally, and spiritually? Do you know what specific gifts you bring to a soul mate? Have you ever made a list of your strengths and weaknesses? When you're looking for your soul mate, you need to be aware of all the best (and worst) you bring to them, because that information will help you know what kind of person will be attracted to you. It will also help you know what kind of person you should be looking for.

I've loved the ongoing discovery of my authentic self, weaknesses and all. I've been able to take off the masks I once wore so people would like me, accept me, hire me, or marry me. An array of personality tests are available, and reputable psychologists can administer most of them. I've taken dozens, including the MMPI (Minnesota Multiphasic Personality Inventory), the Taylor-Johnson Temperament Test, and the Kiersey Temperament Analysis (Meyers-Briggs). All offered valuable information; and each had their weaknesses. I've found that the easiest, most reliable, and most powerful was Florence Littauer's personality test and Dr. Patricia Allen's test for male and female energy.

Personality Plus[3] by Florence Littauer

Florence and her husband, Fred, have taken the original four temperaments theory (first put into practice by the ancient philosopher and physician Hippocrates) and have presented them in an easy-to-understand testing format: *Popular, Powerful, Perfect,* and *Peaceful* personalities. It's fun to take the test and see which of the four personalities best fits you, and how you will naturally attract or repel other personalities.

Popular Sanguine temperaments can liven up a group at any time or in any place with their quick smile, light touch, and amusing outlook. They are optimistic, energized by people, sometimes silly, sometimes sweet, and once in a while they get a little out of control. Every party needs a Popular Sanguine, but don't count on them for perfection.

The *Perfect Melancholy* is the opposite personality. Noted for their artistic, musical, or other creative talents, they are usually more detail oriented than the Popular Sanguines. In a group they're a little more cautious at first. Perfect Melancholy are deep and sensitive, and they love to analyze life. If you want it done just right, you need a Perfect Melancholy.

The other outgoing and optimistic personality is *Powerful Choleric,* who is similar to the Sanguine, but a little more down-to-earth. Powerful Cholerics are outspoken and high energy, can see the big picture quickly, and tend to take charge wherever they are. They seem fearless and are quick on their feet. You want a Powerful for a leader, but be careful—this temperament just might mow you down.

The opposite of the Powerful is the *Peaceful Phlegmatic.* The Peaceful Phlegmatics are the most balanced of all the four temperaments. They are calm, easy-going, kind, generous, helpful, and devoted workers. Their greatest strength is adaptability. They become the life of the party when no Sanguine is around, focus on details when needed, and take charge only if they have to, being careful not to run over anyone. Watch out, though, they control with avoidance and procrastination.

Others have come up with similar studies (using four animals, four colors, four letters, etc.), but the Littauer model is unique in two ways. First, it allows for the understanding of "masked" behavior and responses people wear because of what they were taught to do as children, what society or others expected of them, or what they believed was right and wrong. When these people lose touch with their authentic self, they wear a mask (a persona or false self), and that can affect their test results. Secondly, the Littauer model considers the effect of birth order and other outside influences on one's natural temperament. Oldest children, for example, usually are high achievers or perfectionists because of the pressure of their family position. While some were born with those natural traits, other firstborns were not. Being the oldest might mold one into these characteristics, but because of their natural temperament, some will be energized by the extra pressure (the naturally Powerful or Perfect), and others (The Popular or Peaceful) will be exhausted.

How does this affect your search for a soul mate? Opposites tend to attract, so you will want to know what kind of people will be attracted to you. You'll need to understand what you can expect and not expect from others. You may not want an opposite in some areas, but in other areas you may.

Consider buying the book, *Getting Along with Almost Anybody—The Complete Personality Book* by Florence and Marita Littauer. You can read about the four temperaments and how you fit in. You can even take the personality test, which is included. This tool has improved each of my relationships, from work to friends to romance, and can be so life-changing that I incorporate it into every seminar I give.

The Test for Male and Female Energies

While I don't agree with all her views, Dr. Patricia Allen has formulated a fascinating theory about the passive (Littauer's Peaceful) and aggressive (Powerful) personality models, and offers a valuable assessment tool. In her book *Getting to "I Do,"* Dr. Allen writes about the dynamic in relationships where one is always the "female energy" and one the "male energy," but the roles do not necessarily equate to biological sex.[4] I see now from my own experience, and from those I counsel in divorce groups, that the failure to understand this theory has resulted in the collapse of numerous relationships. Here's an example:

Sarah is an outgoing, high-energy manager of a title company. She's climbing the corporate ladder at breakneck speed, makes a hefty income, and enjoys tennis on the weekends. She's attracted to Jack, a handsome, easygoing computer executive with a brilliant mind and a creative flair, who also likes weekend tennis. They meet, fall in love, and get married. Sarah is happy to have Jack's stable, laid-back attitude, which helps calm her down and gives her balance. When she flies off the handle because of stress, he keeps the boat steady.

Now that they are married, however, Sarah is thinking about children and wants to work fewer hours. She knows that she's been burning the candle at both ends and tells Jack she wants to work part-time. Jack agrees (as he always does), and they begin to live on less income. But Sarah still feels stressed about money and is beginning to resent Jack's lack of energy and his unwillingness to work harder and climb his own corporate ladder. Jack is feeling the pressure, but he needs to leave time for tennis and his woodworking hobby. He does not want to work as intensely as Sarah expects. The babies begin to come, and

Sarah goes back to work. She is bitter because she hoped that Jack would work for a promotion in his company and become the major breadwinner after they were married. But Jack is happy where he is and resents the pressure to perform. Unless they recognize and reconcile their roles, the unmet expectations and distance between them may eventually lead to their divorce.

Sarah is delightedly feminine, but her personality is distinctly male: she makes most of the final decisions in the family, has the higher energy levels, and is quick to find ways to provide, solve problems, and take on the world. Jack is masculine, but his easygoing nature is more female: he is loving, supportive, and willing to let her lead and have her way. Without being a doormat, he respects his wife and defers to her in most areas. In return, she cherishes his warmth and support. Sarah expected Jack to advance to the typical male leadership role once they got married, however, and now she's bitterly disappointed that he didn't.

Individuals can avoid this common pitfall in relationships, Dr. Allen says, by first thoroughly understanding their own personality and desires for a relationship; then choosing the role in which they feel most comfortable before they date. Strong, powerful personality people who prefer to lead and do not readily let go of their control should date others who are willing to be loving supporters, and neither should expect the other to change. Accepting these roles can be difficult, however, in a society that reveres powerful men and equally powerful women, but tends to equate peaceful, supportive deference and passivity with weakness.

By helping you understand yourself, Littauer's and Allen's books and tests help prepare you for healthy dating. In the process, you may need to examine, let go of, and grieve the loss of immature, unrealistic expectations or fantasies. Personal growth is hard work, but it can help you avoid broken hearts in the future.

6. *Social*

One of the best ways to meet a soul mate who shares your interests is to make time to pursue those interests. Social activities are important in becoming a balanced, whole person, and they can help attract like-minded people of both sexes. My friend Patrick, who tends to be an introvert, told me, "I often despair of finding a mate, much less a soul mate. I hate having dinner in front of the TV, but I do, so I don't feel like I'm alone. I realize I have to get out socially, because my soul mate is not going to come walking between me and my TV."

When Frances answered my soul mate survey, she said, "I'm in fact, rather timid about seeking men; to actually seek a partner seems daunting and too much work." I told Frances to ask for God's blessing and then, like Rebekah, go to the "well." After all, Eliezer would never have found Rebekah if she was hiding in her home waiting for an angel of God to knock on the door. God will hear your prayer, bless your search, and inspire the men to seek you out, but you have to make yourself visible and available.

If you're an attorney and want to increase your chances of meeting people who share your interests, you're more likely to find them at a weekend law seminar, not at the swap meet or the mall. Looking for someone who enjoys working with children? Then volunteer as a mentor, a scout leader, or Sunday school teacher. Stay active and involved in social groups or play time activities that attract the kind of person you desire.

Most dating books on the market encourage you to increase your social exposure by participating in a long list of suggested activities: bike rides, gym classes, night courses, museum visits, jaunts to the opera, and tennis matches. I don't know about you, but I have work, laundry, cleaning, shopping, and once in awhile a Jazzercise class. These responsibilities leave me very little extra time. So stay focused and selective with your time and energy and, for heaven's sake, don't exhaust yourself by getting caught up in a performance trip.

7. *Sexual*
This area of life gets a lot of focus but very little healthy formation; lots of talk, but little teaching. Historically,

most parents have been afraid to talk about sex, leaving their children undeveloped and ripe for half-truths, lies, and seduction. Today's children have been abandoned to the government, the medical community, and the schools, who fill their minds with promises of self-gratification as their *right*, forgetting their *responsibility* to society—and to another's heart.

Sex was created for, and works best as, the beautiful expression of love between husband and wife. There's always a hefty physical, emotional, and spiritual price tag when it's enjoyed any other way.

So what do you do to prepare your best gifts in this area? Ask God's blessings in your search for good books, videos, trusted teachers, counselors, and other sources of wisdom about handling this precious personal present. Whatever you do, don't ignore this area and hope everything will be all right in the future. If you love someone, you have a responsibility to know and understand all of that person and be ready for marriage. Some practical things you can do right away include:

- Learn about your own body, if you haven't already.
- Learn how your mind and emotions can lead you to sexual addictions.
- Learn about the opposite sex and their physical makeup and responses.

- Women: subscribe to a balanced magazine for men that talks about their struggles with sex, love, addiction, and pornography. Don't remain ignorant on these issues.
- Men: read about women's whole sexuality so that in your marriage, you can bring your soul mate real love, patience, and understanding.

8. *Spiritual*

Research has shown that spiritual commitment and marital success are closely related. Spirituality is not lighting candles, chanting mantras, singing songs, or contemplating the cosmos. These are only outward physical practices. Intimate knowledge, love, and time with God the Creator will always positively affect your romantic relationship. How?

- When you know God, you know how much you're loved.
- When you feel deeply loved by God, you're not nearly as desperate for love from others.
- When you know God's unconditional love, you can love others in the same way—unconditionally.
- When you become completely vulnerable and intimate with God, you can be vulnerable and intimate with others.
- When you love others, more love comes to you.

Do you want to see how this works? Take a piece of paper and draw a triangle. Write "God" at the top, "Me" at the lower left, and "My Soul Mate" at the lower right. Now, imagine each of the two people moving from the base of the triangle up the sides toward the top (God). Notice as they move up the sides and closer to God, the distance between the two people is shortened and they become closer to each other. However, if one moves closer to God and the other stays in the same place, the distance between the two people is actually widened. When one of you is developing spiritually and the other is not, or at a much slower pace, it can put stress on the relationship. The closer you get to God, the closer you come to each other. It's a deep and complex spiritual principle, but one that you need to understand. Spiritual integration is one of the greatest gifts you can bring to your soul mate.

Know Each Other in the Biblical Sense

When Scripture says a man and woman knew each other, people automatically think that only means sex. But in Bible times, men and women were preparing to know each other in every area of life from the time they were little. Girls learned homemaking skills and how to care for and teach children. As they got older, they were invited into the secret circles of mothers, aunts, and grandmothers to learn all about their bodies, their spirits, their emotions, and sexual intimacy. The older women would explain what they knew about the way men thought and what men needed. Men would similarly train their sons, taking them at adolescence into the male society and teaching them all about themselves, the world, their God, women, and children. By the time they were ready for courtship and marriage, young couples who were still pure and chaste, would know each other in ways that people who have been weaned on junk TV have yet to learn. They didn't know each other sexually, but they did know quite a bit about themselves, the opposite sex, and life in general. Today, singles enter into marriage with a lot more ignorance and a lot less knowledge of life than they should.

Remember to keep balance. Continue to grow to be the best you can be in all areas of your life; breathe, relax, and enjoy each day and the people in it; and trust that God has already heard and answered your prayer for a soul mate.

What Does My Fear Say?

I'm afraid that if I start looking at myself, I will see something I don't like. Then what do I do? Besides, it seems like way too much work. I'm afraid that I'd have to change—and that is scary.

What Does My Faith Say?

If I trust that God will bless me, that means He'll bless me in all areas, even in my attempts to make myself more pleasing, attractive, and ready for true love. I don't have to be afraid of what I see because I am already deeply loved by God, who sees it all (Psalm 139)! I can choose to begin enjoying the discovery of my authentic self.

What Should I Remember?

- *The more inner gifts you bring to another, the richer the relationship will be.*
- *To bring your best to another is an act of true love.*
- *Learning more about yourself helps you make wiser choices.*

7

Step 4:
Look for Things
That Matter

One night I was enjoying a juicy steak dinner in Indian Wells with my girlfriend, Judy, when our married friends, John and Cindy, visited our table. I told John, who's a well-respected, local attorney, that I was writing a new book about soul mates. As I was explaining my emphasis on the initial selection process, he nodded in agreement that it is the most important part of selecting a mate.

"Rose," he said, putting his glass down, "It's just like my court cases. I want to win, but no matter how well I prepare or perform in court, the most important step in my winning is at the very beginning—picking the right people for the jury. I can tell some things about them from their appearance, but I need to spend time asking them a lot of questions to make a wise decision to keep or dismiss them. Sometimes it may take a few days just to pick a qualified jury. The more important the case, the more careful I am with my selection. If I don't carefully screen, interview, and analyze who will be with me throughout the case, I can lose before the judge ever walks into the courtroom."

He smiled at Cindy, who added, "Yeah, be careful when you date an attorney!"

Attorneys or not, smart men understand the need for a plan and a process for picking a soul mate. Take, for example, my grade-school friend, Tom, a plant geneticist. He breeds new varieties of sunflowers for plant and seed sales all over the world. As Tom and I discussed the process of finding the right person to marry, we agreed about the importance of picking character qualities right up front—something Tom does in his business of breeding the perfect plant.

"It's the *initial selection process* that is the most important step in creating a beautiful flower," Tom said. "I can move that flower to a warm or cool environment, feed it, care for it, and try to keep it safe from pests, but if I haven't first selected the basic genetic traits for hardiness it may not survive, no matter how hard I work to save it."

That sounds a lot like marriage. When I take an honest look at my own past failed relationships, I see that no matter how hard I worked, how much I grew or changed, or what steps I took to save the relationship, the failure was usually due to something that was present or missing from the very beginning.

Tom and John are both right. While daily care must be given to sustain the flower of any relationship, or ongoing efforts made to "win our case," our success or failure can be almost totally dependent on our initial choice. Outward appearances are important first indications, but we need to look deeper for things that matter.

What Did Eliezer Look for?

The girl was very beautiful, a virgin; no man had ever lain with her. She went down to the spring, filled her jar and came up again. The servant hurried to meet her and said "Please give me a little water from your jar." "Drink, my lord," she said, and quickly lowered the jar to her hands and gave him a drink. After she had given him a drink, she said, "I'll draw water for your camels too, until they have finished drinking." So she quickly emptied her jar into the trough, ran back to the well to draw more water, and drew enough for all his camels. (Genesis 24:16-20)

Eliezer had a list of the things he wanted to find in a soul mate for his master's son, Isaac. As he watched Rebekah at the well, he made several observations that pleased him:

She was "very beautiful." The ancient Scriptures don't tell us what exactly her beauty was, whether in her face, eyes, figure, the way she carried herself, or all of these. Regardless of the specifics, she was pleasing to the eye. Today society either places too much emphasis on physical beauty, or pretends it doesn't (or shouldn't) matter. It *does* matter to all of us, to some degree or another. Instead of focusing too much or too little on beauty, we need to keep it in balance. We all want someone who is reasonably healthy and clean, smells good, has a sparkle in his or her eye, and a smile. Maybe beauty was first on Eliezer's list of observations because the physical is usually what we see first.

She was single, available, and of good virtue. Next he noticed her social standing, conduct, and character, which also pleased him. In those days the term "virgin" could mean simply a young unmarried woman. The phrase "untouched by man" or "had not lain with man" is sometimes used with "virgin," to indicate that not only was she single and available for marriage, but she also was morally and physically pure and chaste. She had been saving the gift of her body and the powerful heartstrings that come with sex for her one true love. Some singles who have lost their virginity, or have been previously married, downplay the importance of purity because they don't know how to go back to being physically chaste, and therefore feel they have no right to expect it from others. But virgin or not, holding that special part of us aside for just the right person at the right time is attractive to everyone. You have choices, and even if you have had a previous marriage or sexual relationship, you can be determined to stay morally and physically pure until you meet your soul mate.

She was from the people his master considered to be of good stock. Abraham had made it very clear to his servant that he should not go to certain places to select his son's soul mate. He wanted the girl to be of his own "people," whom he knew to be godly and of good character. You, too, need to look for this in potential mates. Location, past history, and family influences can initially mold and continue to influence the character of a future spouse. Parents who are addicted or abusive will physically or emotionally wound their children, who in turn are apt to grow up and pass the same on to their families. You don't always see all of the hidden attitudes, ideals, or beliefs that stem from a family system until you're living with it. Marriages between two people of different races, religions, and family traditions can be burdened with an extra set of problems that are packed neatly in the baggage you bring to the relationship. Since marriage can be difficult, and you don't want to add any additional stress, be honest about how these issues might affect your choice of who to date or not. Talk about these differences with trusted advisors and pray for God's guidance.

She was polite, cheerful, hardworking, and extremely selfless. When Eliezer asked for a sip of water from her pitcher, she didn't question him, hold back, argue, or refuse him. She agreed with what tradition tells us was a kind and loving attitude. In any relationship, whether it's a coworker, family member, or your soul mate, love can only blossom when there is a spirit of giving. That goes much further than beauty in marriage.

Rebekah's next act showed an unusually generous heart. To grasp the extent of her selflessness, you need the following brief course in camelology.

Domesticated thousands of years ago by frankincense traders, the gangly, cud-chewing Bedouin camels are the one-humped variety also known as Arabian camels. These beasts-of-burden became the desert dweller's primary source of transport, shade, milk, meat, wool, and hides. Camels have the reputation of being bad-tempered, obstinate creatures who spit and kick, but with a trusting relationship with their masters they can be patient and intelligent. When they're loaded up and have to rise to their feet, the moaning and bawling sound they make is like the grunting and heavy breathing of a weight-lifter in action, not a sign of resistance to having to work or an expression of pain.

Eliezer's ten camels, fully loaded with supplies and gifts, were undoubtedly tired, dusty, smelly, and thirsty. When they travel through the desert, camels can lose from a quarter to nearly half of their body weight without impairing normal functions, and they can drink up to thirty gallons of water a minute. Such an amount would kill most animals, but the camel's unique metabolism allows it to store water in its bloodstream (not its hump—which is stored fatty tissue). To reduce water loss, their kidneys can concentrate their urine so that it is as thick as syrup and has twice the salt content of seawater.

Now imagine ten fully-grown camels of about 1,500 pounds each, seven feet high, and each with thirty-four sharp teeth that enable it to eat thorny desert scrub. They're at the well and ready to drink their weight in water! To water Eliezer's camels, Rebekah would first have to establish trust and authority with the animals, two desirable character traits I'm sure Eliezer was adding to his mental checklist. Then she'd have to take the reins of each (attached by the small peg, a *khezam,* in their nose) and make them kneel on their front legs to lower their huge mouths into the watering trough. Because of their burdens, care would have to be taken to let them down slowly. Once they began to drink, their back ends would follow into a full kneeling position. As they rapidly consumed hundreds of gallons of water, Rebekah would need to run back and forth from the well with her heavy jar. Even if she gathered some of her sisters or friends to help, the task would take a long time and require a lot of work.

Getting a few buckets would be hospitality (in Hebrew a *mitzvah* or good deed); helping to water a few of the camels would have been generous; but Rebekah's single-minded devotion to the whole task and willingness to serve without being asked impressed Eliezer with the character behind her pretty face. Would you do all that for a stranger for no pay? When was the last time you unselfishly and cheerfully did something difficult for someone without being asked?

You probably can list numerous different reasons why you, or people you know, have failed in their relationships, broken off engagements, or left their spouses. But have you ever stopped to consider that behind each and every reason is a form of selfishness?

What Else Should We Look for in a Soul Mate?

Alan and Kirsten shared their insight on soul mates in Randy Carlson's *Parent Talk* newsletter by answering the question "How do you decide who to marry?"[1]

"You got to find somebody who likes the same stuff. Like, if you like sports, she should like sports, and she should keep the chips and dip coming."—*Alan, age 10*

"No person really decides before they grow up who they're going to marry. God decides it all way before, and you get to find out later who you're stuck with."—*Kirsten, age 10*

Things that matter now can drastically change as one gets older. A forwarded e-mail I received listed what women want in a man in the category of "his looks":

At age 22 we want . . . drop-dead gorgeous
At age 32 we want . . . nice looking (prefer hair on head)
At age 42 we want . . . not too ugly (bald okay)
At age 52 we want . . . keeps hair in nose and ears
                             trimmed
At age 62 we want . . . doesn't scare small children
At age 72 we want . . . breathing

What really matters are characteristics and qualities that will help insure that the love and honor in your relationship survives when tough times come—as they always do. A list of what you want and don't want in a potential mate is necessary for making a smart selection. I call it a grocery list because searching for a soul mate is a lot like shopping for food:

- You should never go shopping if you're too hungry, because you'll probably: (a) buy the first thing you see, (b) buy something that's not good for you, (c) waste your money, or (d) end up buying something that looks good, but tastes terrible when you get home. If you're isolated, lonely, or starved for affection, that neediness can set you up for poor choices.
- You should never go grocery shopping with all your children because they'll try to get you to purchase what they

want. They'll throw tantrums when you ignore them, and they will distract you from making wise choices. You might just throw something in the cart to quiet them, or you'll get frustrated and go home with no groceries. Single parents need to keep a healthy perspective. They can listen to their children, but they must make their soul mate decision on their own and for the right reasons.

- When you go to the store with no prepared list, you'll forget what you really wanted or needed and end up having to do it all over again later. Not planning ahead in your search for a soul mate can keep you stuck in the same cycle over and over again.

- If you know you have a bad habit of spending too much money or making poor choices in the cosmetics, gourmet food, or bakery departments, you simply should avoid going down those aisles. In dating, once you know what you want and don't want, avoid dating someone wrong for you, stay away from unhealthy social groups or places, and don't keep dating the wrong person because you hope they will change. Leave and go down another "aisle."

- If you know specifically what you want ahead of time (like homemade chili with beans), take the recipe with you. You can pick out the exact items you need and the shopping goes much easier. There is no guessing; you don't overspend; and you don't buy items you would waste later. Best of all, you enjoy anticipating the meal while you shop. Making your list and shopping only for those items that you need is the smartest way to "shop" for a soul mate.

We're Young When We Start Our List

Whether it is written down or in our head, we all have a list of what we look for in a potential mate. We're usually aware of some items on our list, while others may be subconscious desires developed when we were children. I remember many of the boys in my first-grade class like it was yesterday, and I still look for some of the qualities I first saw in them:

- Ralph managed to get two cupcakes on hot-dog day (when our mothers brought home-baked treats) and he gave me one. I'll never forget it. *I still look for someone who's willing to share and even sacrifice for me.*
- Daryl drew pictures on the back of his father's architectural blueprints and gave them to me. Each was the same scene: we were the mom and dad standing in front of a house with dogs, kids, flowers, and clouds. *I still look for a man who has a specific vision for the future and wants to share it with me.*
- Tom was quiet, paid close attention in class, and always obeyed. During school, he offered to do the

extra jobs to help the teacher. *I still look for a man who is aware of others, has a heart for helping, and wants to obey and please God.*

- Steve was smart as a whip and handsome to boot. *I still look for a man whom I can admire and respect, and who can turn my knees to jelly.*

Some people never stop to think about what they want in a soul mate, even though they have vague subconscious preferences. Some personalities naturally make lists and analyze people, places, and things. Others have to develop the discipline to think past surface issues, investigate, or write things down. Dr. Gary Lawrence, speaker and author of *Rejection Junkies*, shared the story of his courtship with his wife Sylvia. Gary is a combination of the Powerful and Perfect personalities. He likes to take charge, analyze the situation, make lists of what is good and bad, right and wrong, solve the problem, and move on to the next project. Sylvia is his complete opposite, a beautiful blend of Peaceful and Popular personalities. She's sweet, loving, kind, and almost glides like a swan on the glassy surface of life. Making lists is too much of a bother for Sylvia. Her reasoning goes like this: *Why make lists or look too deep if it would reveal problems or cause conflict?* Sylvia's strength is in her steady support, quiet and enduring love for everyone, and her bright outlook on life. When I asked Gary if he and Sylvia had lists of qualities in mind when they got married thirty-five years ago, he told me:

"I had a list, but Sylvia didn't. I'll never forget taking her out to dinner at a steak house one night where I began in an efficient and businesslike manner asking what qualities she was looking for in a man. She looked at me with those big brown eyes like I was nuts and said she didn't know. When I asked her why not, she said she hadn't really thought about it. I started to get irritated because I wanted her to know I was the man for her. How could I rate in her eyes if she hadn't even made up a scorecard?

"So I asked her if she'd like to marry a man with integrity. She thought a minute and agreed that would be nice. Then I asked if she would like a man who was hard-working and honest. She thought again for a while and then agreed that would be nice, too. From the list in my head, I asked her every single good quality I thought I possessed, and after an hour-and-a-half of me asking and her saying 'that would be nice,' I finally told her, 'Sylvia! *I'm* the man for you!'"[2]

*M*aking a Realistic List

It's a jungle out there, but making your list can help you find your Tarzan or Jane. Dr. Neil Clark Warren suggests making a list of the top twenty-five "must haves" and the top twenty-five "can't stands" for a potential mate before you date. Then, as you're making your lists and feeling pretty satisfied with yourself, he challenges you to reduce each list to ten each "must haves" and "can't stands." He warns that your chance of finding someone that fits all twenty-five "good" characteristics and none of the twenty-five "bad" is slim to none. In his book, *Two Dates or Less,* Dr. Warren says, "A list of ten things you definitely want and ten things you definitely don't want offers a happy medium: you'll be picky enough to insure your mate will be well suited to you, but not so picky that you'll never find someone who can live up to your demands."[3]

What's Wrong with Perfection?

Most people have the mistaken belief that they deserve perfection in a mate. We've been told by the media that we deserve perfection in everything else, but that can tend to set us up for great disappointment or depression because, guess what—life never is perfect. Neither are people. People who have been divorced, or are children of divorced parents, think finding the perfect person will guarantee against another failed marriage. Most people blame their divorce on the imperfection in the other person when that might only be part of the problem. Most children of divorced parents are hoping to avoid the pain their family suffered by holding out for the perfect person. We're all afraid of pain and often will go to any length to avoid it.

Perfection is something that soul mates will be working toward for the rest of their lives, not something they should expect immediately from each other. You need to be careful not to swing too far to the other extreme, however, and tolerate abusive behaviors or settle for less than you really need. You should keep your standards high, but allow the teeter-totter to tilt a little from time to time.

Why You Might Change Your List

I recommend you read Dr. Neil Clark Warren's *Two Dates or Less*[4] because it goes into helpful detail and insight about each character quality. I've made my list and had to revise it a few times; not a problem. Here are the requirements I made when I met and began to date a handsome, outgoing businessman I'll call "Pete":

Have-to-Have	Won't Tolerate
Same Faith	Spiritual Immaturity
Male Energy (Leader)	Financial Irresponsibility
Teachable Spirit	Addictive Personality
Emotionally Balanced	Mentally or Emotionally Lazy
Matched Intelligence	Uses Pornography
Good Communicator	Smoking
Financially Secure	Procrastination
Strong Character	Lack of Cultural Interests
Taller Than Me	Indecisiveness
Likes to Travel	Sports Freak

When I spent time with and observed Pete, he matched every single one of my top ten on both sides. When he made his list and showed it to me, I got a little excited because I felt I fit all of his, too. But apparently I didn't. I was sadly reminded that *when there is no spark, there is no spark*. It doesn't matter if you think you fit someone else's list, or if he/she fits yours; fitting on paper may lack an intangible "chemistry" (sometimes different from sexual chemistry) that will make one person choose to look elsewhere. In my haste to put a person into a perfect little box, I had forgotten about a very important ingredient in my recipe for love: being desired by the other person. After I cried my tears and wiped my eyes, I took out my top-ten list, crossed out "Likes to Travel" and replaced it with "Adores me."

Could Pete and I have developed that spark later in the relationship? Maybe, maybe not. Some certainly do, as I know I have in the past. Who ever really knows? But I do know that as long as I use my head to list what is important; listen for God's voice to know what is right; continue to live each day in love and joy; and trust in God's blessings, I don't have to worry or obsess about anything.

Despite the outcome of my soul mate search, the list-making process is an extremely helpful exercise that got me thinking beyond the surface issues into areas that were important to me. Truthfully, I need to look inside more and pray for added wisdom because, more often than not, I end up listing qualities I want in a false soul mate. A false soul mate is someone who meets the criteria that matches my false self—the role I play, the star I want to be, and the exterior persona I try to show the world.

Let me share a story of two acquaintances. Nancy wants to quit work and live a country club lifestyle. Result: she's looking for a rich golfer. Jennifer has been hung-up on rock stars since she was a teenager and has played the role of a punk band starlet. Result: she's looking for someone who's "extreme" and musical. Nancy has no idea who she really is inside. Neither does Jennifer. Each has focused their energies on what they want to do and where they want to live rather than on discovering who they each are. Both are hopelessly out of touch with their mental, emotional, and spiritual self.

You can't make your list until you know what you need, and you'll never know what you need until you know *who you are*. If you're growing in your understanding of yourself and seeking God's wisdom, you're ready to move ahead.

Getting Started

As a help to making your "grocery list," I've provided an index to get you started. Don't forget to:

- Make your list and add anything else that you think is important.
- Share the list with your friends, family, or counselor and ask for their input.
- Keep working on it until you think it's right for you.
- Use a pencil with an eraser, or a computer with a delete key, because you might end up changing the list as you experience different people and situations.
- Make sure that anyone who is helping you search for a soul mate has a copy of your list.
- After a few dates, or when you think the time is appropriate, share your list with the other person to stimulate conversation and exploration of each other's wants. Ask if they are willing to make their own list and show it to you. If they're serious about looking for a soul mate, they won't object to seeing your list or making one of their own.
- If you discover that person doesn't match your "have-to-haves" or "won't tolerates," think about ending the relationship quickly so that neither one of you gets too emotionally bonded and hurt. Before you end the dating relationship, however, check your concerns with a trusted friend and ask God to send you grace and wisdom to see the truth and do the right thing.

Things I Want and Don't Want in a Soul Mate

Have-to-Have	Won't Tolerate
Clean	Messy
Smart	Uneducated
Financially stable (no major debts)	Can't handle money/ major debts
Good listener	Talks too much
Good self-expressesion	Poor communicator
Peaceful	Too quiet or passive
Strong faith	Undecided faith or spirituality
Loves children	Doesn't like kids
Good personal hygiene	Poor personal hygiene
Open to learning	Refuses help or counseling
Likes to drink moderately	Alcohol abuser
Strong self confidence	Braggart
Will let me lead	Too bossy or controlling
Dresses well	Poor taste in clothes
Cultural interests	No cultural interests
Likes sports	Sports addict
Likes animals	Hates animals
Handsome or pretty	Homely or plain
Healthy and fit	Too fat or too thin

Have-to-Have	Won't Tolerate
Certain height	Too tall or short
Similar intelligence or education	Big difference in intelligence/education
Certain religious denomination	Different religious denomination
Close to me in age	Not close to me in age
Certain race	Certain race
Leading personality (male energy)	Too domineering
Supporting personality (female energy)	Too passive or weak-willed
Makes a good income	Income level too low
Will stay home while I work	Won't stay home while I work
Likes to travel	Stays at home too much
Enjoys or shares my specific hobby	Travels or works too much
Has strong values and principles	Weak values or principles
Has similar political views	Opposite political views
Not afraid of healthy child discipline	Too harsh or too weak with child discipline
Is healthily detached from family	Still tied to family apron strings
Willing to put me first	Puts family, friends, or others first

Have-to-Have	Won't Tolerate
Knows how to fight fairly	Fights with character assaults or withdrawal
Emotionally stable	Prone to depression
Will open up emotionally	Too emotionally guarded/ private
Romantic spark/ chemistry	No romantic spark/ chemistry
Likes to read	Can't or won't read
Shows compassion to self & others	Too critical or harsh with self and others
Listens to and considers criticism	Too defensive
Seeks God's will on a daily basis	Doesn't integrate spiritual beliefs with daily life
Enjoys music	Poor or different musical taste
Is not afraid of commitment	Fearful of making commitments
Can trust easily	Too cautious and untrusting
Punctual	Always late
Wants to solve problems quickly	Avoid conflict or problem solving
Has healthy attitudes about sex	Has sexual problems
Wants children	Doesn't want children
Will put God first over me	Won't put God first

Have-to-Have	Won't Tolerate
Seeks a spiritual mentor	Not open to spiritual growth
Makes more money than I do	Makes more money than I do
Willing to splurge once in a while	Too cheap and chintzy
Is emotionally interdependent	Too dependent or independent
Lack of addictions	Addictions
A smoker	A smoker
A nonsmoker	A nonsmoker
Healthy sexual control	Uses pornography
Has not been previously married/divorced	Has been previously married/divorced
Physically whole	Physical handicap
Has a well-defined career	Has no well-defined career or immediate goals
Can easily show physical affection	Too much public display of affection
Good sense of humor	Doesn't listen well
Willing to be spiritual leader	No interest or skills in spiritual leadership
Willing to pray together	Won't pray together

Can you see that it can take a lot of time and talk to really know if someone meets your criteria? I hope you have fun making your list, and that you'll realize:

(1) Your list doesn't have to be perfect. It's only meant to help you get a little more focused in your search.

(2) It's like a recipe card; you can always add a dash of this or throw in a cupful of that at the last minute, but the basic ingredients should always be there.

(3) Look inside to see if you have developed things that matter in your own life. Use your intellect, intuition, and instincts to look past the surface. This is a skill that will help you in every area of life, for the rest of your life.

*G*reat Expectations

In addition to your list of needs and wants, start thinking about a list of expectations in areas that most couples rarely discuss. Unmet or hidden expectations can pop up when you least expect them and sour a soul mate relationship.

Expectations about life come from watching the way your parents lived or from your family traditions and culture. They sometimes don't show up in the normal dating period. Many of them surround the way you spend your money and your time. One of the men I've dated was madly in love with me (supposedly), so naturally I expected the big rah-rah and huge gifts at Christmas. I assumed he loved the holidays as I did, and I was shocked at his chintzy little presents. I know it sounds selfish and immature (and it was), but I never had stopped to think about how he might view holidays and gift giving. As a start, make your list of expectations around the calendar: work, home, parenting, family relationships, discipline, vacations, and money. Try to anticipate things that would normally happen in the future. For example:

- Do you expect to spend every Thanksgiving at your mother's?
- Do you expect your husband to always stand up against his own parents on your behalf?
- After an argument, do you expect an apology?
- Do you expect your vacation to always be at the same place and same time in August?
- Do you expect your children to attend private school?
- Do you expect your spouse to be available 24/7 because Mom was for Dad?
- How will you handle priority, money, or discipline issues with stepchildren?

Even with great expectations, you never can cover every single situation or circumstance as you hunt for a soul mate, but the more you talk about things that matter, the greater chance you have of making the best selection in choosing your soul mate.

What Does My Fear Say?

I used to think I knew what I wanted, but now I'm afraid I really don't know what to look for. What if my standards are too high or too low? What if I make my list and I never find that person?

What Does My Faith Say?

I can learn from Eliezer. He focused on character, and God blessed him in his search. I just need to stay in touch with what I think God wants for me and I'll be all right.

What Should I Remember?

- *To find what I want, I need to first know what I want.*
- *Making a specific list of "have-to-haves" and "won't tolerates" is an absolute must in my search for a soul mate.*
- *My list should focus on mental, emotional, and spiritual "things that matter."*

❧ 8 ❧

Step 5:
Ask God for a Sign

Then he prayed, "O Lord, God of my master Abraham, give me success today, and show kindness to my master Abraham. See, I am standing beside this spring, and the daughters of the townspeople are coming out to draw water. May it be that when I say to a girl, 'Please let down your jar that I may have a drink,' and she says, 'Drink, and I'll water your camels too'—let her be the one you have chosen for your servant Isaac. By this I will know that you have shown kindness to my master." (Genesis 24:12–14)

When I was little, I loved to see searchlights sweeping rhythmically back and forth in the night sky. Wouldn't it be nice if we looked out one night and saw glistening lights, or a shining star, that directed us right to our soul mate? Eliezer asked God for a specific sign—why can't we?

From the beginning of time, men have sought signs from God, or whatever perceived divinity they worshipped, to ease their fear, worry, or anxiety. Since human nature has not changed, people still look for signs today. Why? We want decisions to be safe and easy, or we want someone else to take responsibility or show us the way. Like children, sometimes we simply want approval or permission for the things we desire. We want assurance that God will help us and not harm us.

Through the ages, God has chosen to give his people signs and wonders, some of which have been natural and some supernatural. Natural signs can be harder to detect and require more wisdom, while supernatural signs are much more obvious. We usually want supernatural signs because they are easier to read. When it comes to asking God for signs, however, I think we need to remember:

- God still can and does reveal the future and give supernatural signs to certain people at certain times, but he also gives an abundance of natural signs to all of us every day. Maybe you just aren't seeing them. Have you ever wondered why you got that precise telephone call at just a certain time of day? Or why you were chosen for the promotion over others? Or why that nice man that seemed interested never did call you back? You need to develop sensitivity in reading the daily, small signs—rather than hoping for the big ones!

- Most people view signs in one of two extremes: They leave everything up to God expecting a super-spiritual sign to lead the way, and they never use their common sense. Or they try to figure out everything themselves, doubting God's grace and guidance. Both types of people remain insensitive to, and ignorant of, the signs that are all around them.

- Relying on a sign more than relying on God himself can be a form of idolatry, that is, the gift becomes more important than the Giver. Look to God first and don't become absorbed in an unhealthy curiosity about signs. Let the Lord take the lead when it comes to signs—your responsibility is to trust Him.

* * *

Most of society doesn't care where signs come from, as long as they make life easier or confirm their desires. Humans still practice idolatry in many forms. Some common forms of idolatry include:

Divination: The seeking of the future or looking for direction in a way that is unrelated to God. Examples include fortune telling, palm and tea readings, tarot cards, omens, sorcery and witchcraft, horoscopes, ouija boards, and late-night television clairvoyants. Even some practices within respected religious denominations can be nothing more than voodoo spirituality if they are not really from God. Being overly concerned with wanting to know or see the future often indicates that people don't trust God. In relying on these kinds of signs, people reveal their lust for control over time, other people, the future, and even hidden powers from a demonic dimension. These practices contradict the honor, respect, trust, and loving fear owed only to God.

Superstition: The misplaced feelings of honor, reverence, or awe that should normally be felt with authentic worship. One common superstitious practice today is the wearing or displaying of signs, stars, crosses, or other symbols in an effort to ward off evil spirits, rather than as a sign to others of one's relationship with God. The symbols should be like wedding rings—they simply let others know of one's love and commitment to someone. Symbols or rituals should show an outward sign of one's inner respect for God. Such devotions, when rooted in a genuine relationship with God, can help to bring earthly elements into a whole-person experience of the Lord. But wearing or performing something out of fear that God will punish a person for some sin, or as a guarantee that that person will find his or her soul mate, assumes that the act itself will gain one some favor. That is superstition and an affront to God. To attribute the effect of one's prayers or practices to their mere outward performance, apart from one's inner relationship with God, is to be superstitious.

Spiritual Negotiation: Trying to cut a deal with God. The first commandment, to have no other God before Him, clearly condemns any practices of tempting or bargaining with God, or the buying and selling of spiritual things. Demanding that God show you His will by making the red light turn green, expecting He will arrange your promotion at work because you gave generously at church, or showing you a supernatural sign when your soul mate arrives, is a form of spiritual negotiation.

What Others Said about Signs

When I surveyed singles about signs, very few thought asking for signs was a reflection of weak faith, and all were hopeful that God would show them some sign or at least a feeling or confirmation. Some received clear signs while others thought they had no answer from God whatsoever. In the following sampling of replies, you'll see that many singles don't trust their own ability to make wise choices. Could that be a *sign* that singles need to start developing a closer, stronger relationship to God?

"I have not asked God for confirmation because when I have in the past, I admit I manipulated the situation. I believe God does give signs, but if we ask for one right at the beginning (of a relationship), it's like we're not using the brains God gave us. Instead of a sign, I have asked God for discernment."—*Frances*

"I don't think it is a sign of weak faith to ask God for one, since he has always given them to us. But they are not like we think. Sometimes in my dreams the answers come to me; sometimes I see signs in people and circumstances. I have also seen signs in church, in nature, and in Scripture. I know feelings and emotions can be deceiving. I just don't want to have fantasies and obsessions."—*Arlene*

"I think God sends signs but we don't see them. The flood story about the man who ignored the signs changed my mind about this subject. He was on his rooftop in a huge deluge, calling to God for help. Along came a rowboat, then a helicopter, and then the Coast Guard. Each time he told them to go away and leave him alone because God was going to save him. When he finally drowned and was standing at the pearly gates, he asked God why he had not saved him. God answered that he'd sent help three times. I think we don't see the normal signs because we are looking for burning bushes."—*Shelley*

"God gave me a confirmation. I tried to use my head in picking the right kind of man, and I thought I had been pretty careful, but I just wanted to know I had God's blessings. I asked for my future husband to quote a certain

Scripture, and the day we picnicked in the park and he proposed, he read it to me. I knew it was my sign. We're happily married now."—*Jill*

"I asked for signs in the past, and thought I got them, but evidently I was wrong. The relationships I had were not 'the one.'"—*Gina*

"I think God does send signs, and they could be critical in making the right choice. I have prayed, 'Please let this be the one,' but in relationships I haven't asked God for one because I don't trust my receptivity to such a sign."—*Charlotte*

"I don't ask God for signs because it's almost like an indication of our impatience. I don't believe in signs, but I have felt confirmations. The heart is very deceptive. I think seeking God is more important than seeking his signs."—*Dawn*

"I have asked God to let me know if I was making another mistake, to give me a feeling or some kind of a sign, some indication. I had made so many mistakes in the past; I couldn't stand another one. I think I asked him to send a sign because I didn't trust myself. He didn't."—*Kim*

"I think we have to become sensitive to God's leading. I'm not sure about all this sign stuff, but I do know you have to ask God for wisdom . . . which He promises to send us if we ask."—*Nicki*

"I prayed and gave it lots of time to make sure this man was what was best for me. But I also asked for a sign, just to give me some extra confidence. I asked for yellow roses. On the day I knew I had to finally decide, I took an unusual route home from work and walked through an old alley. On the top of a pile of trash were fresh cut yellow roses. I couldn't believe it. Then I stopped for coffee and noticed a small yellow rose in the bud vase on my table. Every other table in the restaurant had red roses. Only mine was yellow. So I've been married to Rowland now for over fifty years."—*Rosemary*

"Some people think the time in history for signs is over. I don't see where there is any proof of that. I don't think God would expect us to make smart choices and then not give us what we need to make them. There are many instances in Scripture where God sent signs to show His authority and His support. I won't make any important decisions without consulting him."—*Rachel*

A Trip to Soul Mate City

I know that God still sends signs, but if you're like most people, you may have been too busy, distracted, or stubborn to see and hear them. Imagine you're in a car traveling through Soul Mate City. Like a Great Engineer, God has designed the network of streets you follow in your relationships, and he's pre-wired your car with intellect, emotions, common sense, intuition, conscience, and other spiritual sensors. Some streets are safe, others are not, and on some you need to proceed slowly and with caution. You'll see red lights and green lights; orange cones; yield signs, caution signs, and stop signs. Have you ever experienced any of these common relationship signs?

Jim and Nancy are dating, but he feels uneasy and even angry when Nancy keeps refusing to talk about her past. That's a clear sign for Jim that Nancy tends to avoid the unpleasant, has little or no trust in him, needs to hide things or keep secrets, and is afraid of developing emotional intimacy. Will Jim listen to the signs his mind and body are sending? Should Jim proceed? Only with caution!

Paul and Rachel work with each other, share common interests, and have developed a deep friendship, including calling each other at home. Rachel wears a blinking "red light" on her left hand: a wedding ring. That's a clear sign that Paul needs to make a U-turn!

Marco and Rita enjoyed a lovely dinner. Now Marco is racing Rita home at thirty miles over the speed limit. Rita is holding tightly to the car seat and begging Marco to slow down, but he just laughs and assures her he's a safe driver. He's ignoring signs that she's afraid. Will she ignore the huge red sign on the odometer that he is selfish, immature, and even willing to risk her life? If he's handsome and she's lonely, she just might.

Jackson and Jody never fight, and Jody brags that Jackson is the kindest and most sensitive man she has ever met. Because of his love and devotion, Jody knows that Jackson truly loves her. When she said she wanted to save sexual intimacy for marriage, Jackson respectfully agreed and never discusses it. Their wedding date is set for June, but Jody still wonders why Jackson has never even tried to kiss her. She also feels uneasy at times because it seems that Jackson's best friend, Jamal, is always with them. Real or imagined, Jody needs to look at the signs.

Trisha and Jason are falling in love. Everyone loves Jason, but Trisha's parents are concerned about his lack of religious background. They raised their daughter in a tightly-knit church community. Jason knows Trisha is devout and prioritizes her close relationship with God. Even though she has always wanted a husband who shared her faith, Trisha doesn't worry because Jason is basically a good person. She hopes that someday after they are married, especially with her setting an example for him, he will start to go to church with her. Trisha sees the sign (dead-end ahead), but ignores it, hoping to find another way because she doesn't want to slow down or take another route.

Sarah and Jeff met at a friend's party. They have spent several dates and long hours talking about what they want in a soul mate. So far, they are in perfect agreement. They have similar interests, their parents know each other, and Sarah's hoping Jeff's the one. She likes everything about him, except his friends. They all show the outward signs of being part of the drug culture, but since she has never seen any of them take drugs; she hopes they just dress that way. Jeff admits he took drugs back in high school, but he's clean now. Yet he still likes to party with the same old people. Sarah's friends want her to wake up and see the (red) light!

Dennis and Tracy are engaged. Dennis tries to ignore all the new clothes Tracy buys weekly. He's concerned about her preoccupation with jewelry. They haven't really talked about money issues because Tracy works and apparently pays her bills. Dennis, who is easygoing and fearful of conflict, just hopes she will live within a budget once they are married. Dennis is driving with blinders on.

Maria and Jesse have been dating for six months, and so far Jesse has only hit Maria twice. He had been drinking both times, and she admits that she was at fault for doing things that she knew would make him angry. Other than that, they are happy and plan to marry next year. Slam on the brakes, Maria, and get out of the car!

* * *

God has proven in many ways that He is here to help, guide, and teach, but He usually doesn't do for an individual what he or she needs to do for himself or herself. God made fat little worms as food for baby birds, but He doesn't throw them into their nest each morning. If you want a sign, you need to use the gifts God has made available to you—stop, look, and listen.

$\mathcal{R}$omeo's Red Flags

Some superstitious people look for signs in tea leaves, but recently I found them in coffee grounds. When an outgoing, confident business associate began to pursue me, I accepted his invitation to Starbuck's. We laughed and shared a little small talk, and I appreciated it when he got right to the point. "Rose, I'm looking for Ms. Right. What are you looking for?"

His blunt question gave me a chance to be open and honest early, so we could avoid an extended dating game. I could tell, he too, was looking for signs: Was I an emotionally available woman? Was I open and honest? Did I know what I wanted and was I able to express it? Was what I wanted compatible with what he wanted? Although it takes more time than one coffee date to discover all the things we need to know about each other, I thought he was smart to start early.

So I answered, "I'm glad you asked. I'm not into dating just for fun, and I'm not looking for a boyfriend. If I do develop a significant relationship with a man, it will be with the intention of marriage."

Using the "m" word on a first date is pretty assertive, but he asked and I answered. To lighten it up a little I added with a grin, "So how much money do you make?" We both laughed.

Like little boys who flex their muscles in front of the girls, my date was eager to share what he could bring to a relationship. I could tell he valued his ability to solve problems and come up with win-win solutions, and he wanted to see if I appreciated that too. He began to quiz me. "Let's say we were ready to order take-out food and watch a video. You wanted Chinese and I wanted Mexican. What would we do?"

"Well," I smiled, "I would probably first try to charm you into Chinese (I stopped and actually batted my eye-lashes), but if I saw that you really wanted Mexican, I would let go and agree on enchiladas."

He didn't seem to like my answer, and immediately I thought I knew why. To keep their man happy, many women give in to his needs and desires so often that they eventually develop an inner resentment. This type of woman keeps giving and giving and giving while the man hasn't a clue of what's going on, *until she blows*. Have you ever asked your date, "Where do you want to go?" and he or she responds, "I don't care; whatever you want to do." Sometimes people (men or women) really don't care, but often it indicates that they are not in touch with or able to express their needs. They let other people make all the decisions and they avoid responsibility. They have not developed assertive skills. Men or women who function in this extreme may be trying to maintain a low level of conflict, sustain agreement, and avoid rejection. It's actually the way they control the situation or the relationship. They usually give in because the other person, who has assumed the role of decision maker, is more openly controlling and prone to irritability or anger.

Sure enough, my date described his previous failed relationships in which this passive pattern had been present. He hated it.

"I'm definitely not afraid to say no or ask for what I want," I said smiling. "It's just that I know I can have Chinese another time. Dinner is not a matter of morals or ethics, and I would get genuine pleasure out of deferring to the wishes of someone I cared about."

I don't think he even heard me. He was too eager to let me know he had the perfect solution. His answer to the hypothetical dinner dilemma was that he would be willing to go out and make an extra trip to get both Mexican and Chinese. I listened carefully to his reply, considered his point, and agreed that could be a good option some of the time. Every woman likes a man who's willing to go the extra mile for her, but maybe he was really only going the extra mile to get what he wanted.

"Would you ever be willing to just give in and eat Chinese?" I asked.

He stared at me like I was stupid and then replied stiffly, "Why should I give in when we could both easily get what we wanted?"

"Well," I asked, "haven't you ever practiced just letting go and pleasing the other person for no other reason than to be less self-centered?"

Forget the ethnic food; now my date was looking at me like I was speaking Russian.

"I go out and make a separate trip for your Chinese food, and you think that's self-centered?" he asked sarcastically.

Uh-oh. Now it was personal and it was my chop suey. I could tell he was getting hot while our coffee (and our date) was getting cold. He changed the subject; we finished with light chitchat and politely shook hands as we left. I never saw him again.

The more we'd talked that night, the more signs I'd seen about his potential to be a soul mate. My restaurant Romeo probably thought I was a wimp for being willing to give up my own way, and at the same time too argumentative for not agreeing with him. While I genuinely admired his desire to be honest, direct, and solve problems, the red flags were stacked up against him:

- He projected his fears of past relationship patterns on to me without verifying that I was the same or different than those other passive women.
- He didn't stop to listen, consider, or find any validity in my point of view.
- His body language and tone of voice were subtly shaming.

- His listening skills were limited; he didn't stop to check that what he thought he heard was really what I meant.
- He was ultimately unwilling to deny himself as long as there was some way to get what he wanted.
- He seemed to view meeting another's needs mostly as a responsibility and a way to avoid later repercussions, rather than as an act of love.

The signs for me were clear, especially the one that read, "Single Lane Ahead."

Eliezer's Sign

In his search for Isaac's soul mate, Eliezer asked God for a very specific sign: He wanted the girl who would be the best choice to agree to serve him and also offer to water his camels. He must have figured that this would be the ultimate test of character, showing a generous spirit and giving heart. There weren't many respectable opening lines a man could use with a young maiden at the well, except a common request for assistance. So Eliezer wanted this to be the chance to get right down to business and see inside the girl's heart. As Abraham's head servant, Eliezer must have been extremely efficient. As with his other tasks, in this special quest he wouldn't want to waste time striking up casual conversation with as many young girls as possible, or spending days getting to know them. He got right to the point by asking Rebekah if she would go out of her way to do something nice for a stranger. Then he *listened* to her reply, *observed* her demeanor, and *verified* her attitude as he watched her. When she was done, he *expressed* his additional needs for a place to stay. If she had said no, I think Eliezer would have quickly moved on to the next potential bride. You'll notice that Eliezer did not ask for some unusual or unrelated omen, such as the water turning purple, the temple horn (shofar) to start blowing, or the camels to start bawling in unison when the right one would appear. The sign Eliezer asked for was Rebekah's character to be immediately and clearly revealed.

The Ways God Shows Us His Signs

If you want to develop sensitivity to the signs that may be leading you to your soul mate, you can begin to use the gifts God has already given you:

By Talking With Each Other. Talking with each other can open avenues where many signs will be revealed. When you're looking for a soul mate, you need to spend more time talking about the things that matter and less time in activity such as watching television, sitting in movies, going to parties, or other pastimes that are fun and healthy but not conducive to long talks, intimate questioning, and sharing. Be brave and don't avoid the scary subjects.

Over Time. While God has designed human nature to reveal itself, you don't always get to see what you want when you want. Some people hide their true feelings, thoughts, or opinions, and only over time will the signs of their character be readily visible. You have to be willing to wait and watch, and allow time to present the perfect moment for your sign.

In Prayer. In prayer you talk to God, but your conversation with Him also should include quiet times where you learn to listen. In quiet moments of listening, God's grace can quicken your senses to a dangerous situation, or give you an intuitive feeling about someone. You also can be filled with a deep sense of His peace that passes all understanding. Sometimes your damaged or fleeting emotions can trick you into false feelings, but a consistent seeking of God's grace through prayer can help you see the real signs.

Through Your Physical Senses. The way your body responds to certain people or situations can signal that something is not right. If you're tired, drained, lethargic, nervous, nauseated, sweaty, prone to tears, or subject to stomach pains, cramps, headaches, chills or other physical signs when you're around someone, your body may be trying to tell you something important that your mind has been ignoring.

Through Dreams. When you don't listen, or your world is too noisy to hear or see signs, your dreams might provide a warning. God frequently allowed truths to be revealed to Old Testament figures in their sleep. If your dreams are disturbing, they may be pointing to fears that your relationship has triggered. If your dreams are peaceful, they might be confirming a wise path.

Through Life. Opening your heart, focusing your mind, and being alert to life can make you aware of signs and wonders all around you. Since I have entrusted myself to God's leading in every area of my life, my eyes and ears are open to miracles, even small ones. I'm always looking!

* * *

Everyone has an opinion about signs from God, but most agree that he created many different ways to send and receive them. Signs I've received from God have included:

- A deep sense of peace that can't be rationally explained
- Disappearance of doubts, worries, and fears
- Doors that open, without me forcing them
- A cooperative response from other people

Instead of waiting for shooting stars, burning bushes, or even yellow roses, keep your eyes open for the special sign God has just for you.

What Does My Fear Say?

What if signs and wonders are a thing of the past? I'm afraid that God won't send me a sign in my search for a soul mate. Sometimes I don't know if I even really believe God cares.

What Does My Faith Say?

I choose to believe God cares. I also choose to start developing my sensitivity to spiritual things so that I can see and hear what God is trying to tell me. I will start right now by praying for wisdom.

What Should I Remember?

- *I need to grow past the need for superstitious signs.*
- *Signs are all around me; I just have to learn how to see and hear them.*
- *God has gifted me with intellect, intuition, and instinct to read signs in my search for love.*

⌘ 9 ⌘

Step 6:
L.O.V.E. Each Other

The Twinkie Theory

In the DivorceCare groups I facilitate in the Palm Springs, California area, we inevitably discuss dating after divorce. People of all ages who come for counseling almost always express their fears about making another mistake in selecting a potential mate. "The divorce was bad, but being thrown back into the dating game is worse," shared Judy, a willowy forty-nine-year-old blonde. She added, "There are so many weird people out there. How can you tell? What do you have to do to know who they really are? I guess I just don't trust my instincts."

Nancy, a sad divorcee in her early forties, offered her insight. "You know, Judy, you are right. I don't always listen to my gut either. In fact, my dog would probably be smarter than me. I mean, if I was standing in front of an elevator, and the door opened and a gnarly, suspicious looking man was standing there, I would probably just get in and hope that he wouldn't kill me!" She added, "But a dog would stop, growl, and refuse to go in. Maybe I should be more like the dog."

We all laughed but realized we'd hit on an important principle. God has given us instincts, intuition, and intellect, and we're supposed to develop and listen to them in times of trouble. Dogs listen to their instincts, we don't. Dogs absolutely will not go where they sense danger. Instead of checking out a situation and listening to our instincts, we've been told by parents, teachers, peers, the media, society, or whomever else we listen to, *not* to listen. Maybe we have listened but then have been shamed or rejected. Most of the ladies in our group reluctantly admitted they probably would have gotten into the elevator because:

- They didn't want the man to think they thought badly of him.
- They viewed it as their duty to be nice to everyone regardless of what they see.
- They didn't want any observers to feel they were weak or scared.
- They didn't want to make the effort to find another way down to ground level.

- They didn't want to be perceived, even by themselves as cold, calculating, or cautious.
- They had not learned to listen to their fears. Instead they hoped against hope that everything would be okay.

Even the men at our DivorceCare meeting admitted to those same reasons for not listening to the inner instincts that God gives for protection and direction, especially in relationships. As we continued to talk about dogs, Eddie shared about his little longhaired Chihuahua, Twinkie.

I asked, "Eddie, let's say Twinkie had eaten a nice lunch, and you threw a dinner steak laced with rat poison down on the floor. What would she do? Would she eat it?"

Eddie gave me a funny look. "No, she'd look at it first, and then smell it. Maybe she'd lick it, but probably not," Eddie replied, obviously wondering where this was going. "She wouldn't eat it."

"Well, what if Twinkie had not eaten for six whole days and was starving, and you threw a poisoned steak down in front of her. What would happen?" I asked.

Eddie hesitated, and then said that Twinkie probably would sniff it for a second, but then gobble it down anyway. I could tell Eddie was sad at the very thought of poor little Twinkie dying on his kitchen floor, but I wanted to make a point.

"If you're lonely and love-starved, you'll be much more prone to gobbling up something that is bad for you, even if you've developed good instincts and a strong conscience," I said, and the group all nodded knowingly. "The key to staying away from poisoned relationships is to develop good instincts, make a thorough investigation first, and make sure you never get too emotionally starved. In fact, let's call it The Twinkie Theory." Everyone laughed and agreed that since the meeting had now "gone to the dogs," it was probably time to go home!

The next week, we got a surprise when Eddie walked in holding the tiniest little furball, tenderly tucked in the crook of his arm. It was Twinkie! Eddie put the dog down on the floor, and we all watched as Twinkie looked, sniffed, and checked each one of us out, keeping a safe distance until she felt comfortable. Then she licked our hands and nuzzled our feet, testing how safe we might be. By the end of the night, we were all fighting to hold Twinkie.

In your relationships, you too, should keep a safe distance while you check things out. If you do, you will eventually—when the time is right—be able to love and be loved without fear.

A Waste of Time

Juan and Cyndy spent lots of time together but never really checked each other out to see if the relationship was safe. They worked at the same company and dated for over a year before they decided to get married. During that time the couple spent several days or nights a week together, and almost every weekend. They went to parties, met each other's families, and thought they got to know each other well. Each knew the other's favorite color, meal, and movie, but neither of them was aware of the other's attitudes about things that mattered. Since they got along so well, they were afraid to bring up any subject that might cause controversy. So they didn't.

Shortly after their wedding, Juan and Cyndy began to discover they had completely different attitudes about money, holidays, church, in-laws and other family members, working on weekends, and how to discipline their children. They fought, gave each other the silent treatment, withdrew, made-up, and fought again. The cycle continued, with the angry times lasting longer than the good times. After five years and two children, they divorced.

Juan told me, "I was so happy when we were dating and didn't want to lose her. I figured there were things that might cause problems, but I didn't want to look too deeply. I was sure that no matter what issues came up after we married, we could talk things out, and I could get her to see things my way."

Cyndy's side wasn't much different. "I was having so much fun, and my last relationship had been so hard, I just wanted it to be easy. I didn't want to check things out. I figured we'd gotten along great for over a year, so I took that to mean that we'd be fine."

When I asked both of them what they would do differently next time, they both agreed they would make better use of their dating time to probe, question, investigate, and dig up as much as they could about the other person. They also would listen to their conscience.

Although it's smart to give our relationships time, we can either waste that time or make wise use of it. If we're blinded by romance, infatuation, or lust, it won't matter how much time we have; we'll miss the signs. When I counsel divorced singles in our DivorceCare program, I tell them that when we date we usually look at each other through romantic, *rose-colored glasses*, ignoring each other's weaknesses. But after the wedding, we start picking each other apart with our *magnifying glasses*. It should be the other way around. Before marriage, we need to use our magnifying glasses to make sure we know exactly what we're getting, and then after marriage, put that magnifying glass away and look at each other lovingly through the rose-colored lenses. Ignoring someone's faults after marriage is real love and helps the marriage last. Ignoring them before is incredibly irresponsible.

What People Think about "Knowing"

I'm always a little surprised to hear what I consider high school beliefs coming from middle-aged and even senior singles. In my soul-mate survey, I asked, "How will you know if someone is your soul mate?" Many younger never-marrieds and older, divorced, or widowed singles responded with the following comments:

"You'll just know." Really? If I were going to interview ten new employees for a position in my company, would I just know who was right? If I spent time chatting with them, I might get a better preliminary idea of who they were and maybe a feel for one over the other. But if I didn't want major problems six months into our relationship, I would be smart to check their resumes, call their references, and have them complete an application, a questionnaire, and a personal interview. As I narrowed down the choices, I might even have them come back a second or third time. It doesn't sound romantic, but you should run your love life a little more like a business.

"Your heart will tell you." Tell me what? How good it feels or doesn't feel? Feelings are fleeting and fickle; they can change in a heartbeat. Are you willing to entrust your heart with a decision that will affect every part of the rest of your life? If it says that person is the one, but his or her probation officer, your pastor, and your parents all disagree, to whom will you listen? God gave you a head and a heart so that you could use both.

"God will show you." I hope that you've already realized that God can lead you, but He also expects you to use your mind, emotions, intuition, and conscience, and to

rely on wise counsel. God can show you only if you're looking, which means asking, questioning, talking, and double-checking. He has His part, you have yours.

"Time will tell." If you have a watch on, stop and look at it for one complete minute. Time continued on while you were sitting there, but what did you learn? Did time tell you anything? Time is only the vehicle that allows you to gather information, but in and of itself, it tells you nothing. You might stare blindly at a television together for two hours, or you can talk about things that matter with your date. Those two hours will pass regardless of how you use them. Time doesn't tell, people tell. You have to listen to them, observe their actions, verify what you think you see and hear, and express yourself to get feedback.

When Sex Is Involved

What happens to the process of getting to know one another when sex is involved? Sex can be magical, mystical, and full of delightful mystery. It's consuming, addictive, and hypnotic. It blinds you and binds you, which is just how God planned it . . . for couples inside the commitment and covenant of marriage. If sex enters the picture when two people are dating, the careful, thorough, investigative process flies right out the window. Once you cross over the emotional or physical sexual boundaries that God has put in place for unmarried people, you lose all perspective. Your focus is blurred, your insight blinded, and your judgment marred. You're giddy with the wine of passion, and like a drunk driver behind the wheel, you ignore red flags, screaming sirens, and the train that is coming down the tracks. It doesn't matter how much time you spend, how many questions you ask, or what steps you're taking to get to know each other, sex changes everything—and not for anyone's good. Do each other a huge favor and follow God's plan for dating and courtship. There will be many years ahead of deep, passionate lovemaking. Keep a clear head for now.

If you want to find someone you can L.O.V.E., start with this simple, four-part plan to use your dating and waiting time wisely: Listen, Observe, Verify, and Express yourself.

Listen to Them

Do you know how hard it is to listen? Because of our natural personalities and the social factors that shaped us, most couples include one who is the better talker and one who is the better listener. While both are necessary for good communication, we can tend to carry either to an extreme. In fact, if one person is extremely quiet, the other person often subconsciously will talk even more to bring balance. If one person is normally expressive, he or she may become much more quiet if someone else is dominating the conversation.

Listening isn't just passively and politely paying attention. Listening doesn't mean we have to agree with someone, but it does mean we quiet our own thoughts to be open to others. When we listen we decrease our self-focus and increase our focus on the other, caring about what they're saying. We slow down and look for the feelings that their words might reveal or conceal.

Because we're all naturally selfish, it's hard work to be a good listener. Like anything else it's a mental and emotional habit we have to develop; it's a labor of love.

When I was growing up, I felt like no one listened to me, so I spent a large part of my adulthood talking so people would listen. Now that I know how much I am loved and accepted and how much God listens to me, I don't need others quite as much. Instead, I try to empty myself and give them the listening (love) that I didn't get as a child.

Some people with quiet personalities almost pride themselves on being good listeners, but it's possible they're sitting too comfortably in their silence and not expressing themselves enough. Perhaps they would rather listen than talk because they fear conflict, chaos, or rejection. For them, it's easier to listen, as they can stay more private and protected. Sometimes they haven't really expended the energy or taken the time to formulate their own thoughts or opinions, or they simply don't care. While some of us chatterboxes have to work hard at being quiet and listening, others have to be willing to make the effort, take the risk, turn off the television or computer, and open up. Listen for the other person's tone of voice. Do they whisper timidly most of the time? Maybe they are fearful and insecure. Are they whiny? Maybe they are extremely self-centered. Are they loud and obnoxious? Maybe they need to be the center of attention. Does their tone of voice change with certain people? Maybe they are rude. Do they talk down to children or members of the opposite sex? Maybe they feel superior. Listen for attitudes of caring and compassion. Listen for an ability to express oneself clearly, openly, and honestly. Listen to your friends and family. Listen to your parents, pastor, or counselor. And don't forget to listen to your conscience.

Observe Them

The next step in finding L.O.V.E. is to observe the people you date. Watch how they treat other people in a store or at a restaurant. How do they treat the waitress? How do they treat older people? How do they deal with children? Do they open doors for others? Do they offer to help, speak up for injustice, and get involved in social or community causes? Do they go the extra mile or just put in the bare minimum? Do they cheat just a little, tell white lies, or keep the incorrect change they got back from the clerk? Do they talk back to their superiors? Do they treat their parents and family with respect? Do they do what they say they are going to do?

How do they dress? How hard do they work? Are they compulsive or addicted? Where do they live? What kind of car do they drive? Where do they work? What do they do? You'd be surprised how many people think these things are not important. As humans, we tend to function in extremes; some place too much importance on cars, money, looks, and careers, but others completely ignore these important indications of character. No matter how handsome, moral, or loyal a man is, if he can't hold a job longer than six months, his wife will have difficulty being married to him.

Never assume that because someone comes from a similar background, race, age group, or religion that they have the same ideals, character, or morals that you have. If you love them, you might project onto them things that aren't really there. Keep your eyes open and the magnifying glass clean.

Verify What You Think You Heard or Saw

Next, confirm what you observe. One of the worst mistakes you can make in assessing others is to assume you know what they said, what they meant, or that they truly are who they appear to be.

Frankie thought she took all the right steps in her dating relationship with her ex-husband. She asked him a million questions about things that mattered and listened carefully to him as he shared what he felt and thought. She asked about his religion, his business, and his past. The only thing she forgot was to *verify* what she heard and saw. After they married, she discovered that he lied to her about his company, and he attended church only when she did. She also regretted that she had not contacted his ex-wife to confirm facts about the past. Frankie loved him and wanted to trust him, so she did.

When you're getting to know someone, you certainly don't have the time and energy to check every single fact and you don't want to be paranoid. You have to be able to trust others, especially those with whom you think you're falling in love. But in reality, life is not perfect and people (even presidents) lie. In looking for love, you need to find a healthy balance of verifying the facts and letting go of your worries. That's where God's gifts of intuition, intellect, and instinct come in handy.

One way to verify what you think you hear or understand is to use simple techniques, called mirroring and clarifying, which many advisors teach in marriage counseling. You simply listen carefully to what the other person tells you, and then before you formulate your reply or opinion, you either clarify or mirror back what you think you heard. This gives the other person a chance to give you more information, confirm that you did understand correctly, or to clarify. This technique can keep you from jumping to conclusions and can benefit any relationship.

* * *

Here's an example of a man and woman at a restaurant on their first date using this method:

Man: I think women should stay home and not work.

Woman (clarifying): Do you mean you think all women should stay home and not work or, that if you were married, you'd like your wife to stay home?

Man: Well, I guess some women like to work, but no one in my family ever did. I think it's up to the men to work and the women to raise the kids.

Woman (clarifying): Do you mean you would never want your wife to work?

Man: Well, no, she could work, as long as she still had time for me.

Woman (mirroring): What I think you are saying is you're used to the woman not working, and you'd prefer your wife to stay home. But if she wanted to work, you would not object as long as there was balance and she had time for you. That you would be a priority—is that right?

Man: Exactly! (Boy, she's brilliant. I should keep this one.)

* * *

Let's say this same woman, who might have been dominated by a parent, a controlling ex-husband, or a boyfriend, had projected her own past experiences onto her date without clarifying. She might have prejudged him, shut down, politely finished her dinner, and never returned his calls again.

What We're Afraid to Verify

We're most afraid to verify sex and money issues. In the soul-mate survey I gave, I was initially surprised that people balked at verifying anything to do with sexual or financial history. Since sex, money, and religion are the three biggest areas of arguments between couples, I realized that people don't want to find out anything that might cause them to reject the other person or to be rejected.

When I started to date again after my divorce, I was shocked to discover the rampant rates of sexually transmitted diseases that prevail in singles of all ages. Millions of good people have had more than one sexual partner and, as a result, are now carriers of herpes, genital warts, or worse. Your soul mate may have a heart of gold and a spirit of truth, but may be harboring infections that can cause you pain, suffering, or infertility for the rest of your life. Before marriage, you both need to undergo a full physical screening, not only as good stewards of your body, but as a gift for the other person. Most of the men surveyed agreed this was smart. But the majority of women were incredibly naïve; they did not want their romantic vision of a soul mate soiled by any hint of reality. Here are some of their comments regarding sex and finances:

Q: *Would you require your soul mate to be tested for all STDs before marriage?*

A: No, I never have and can't imagine that I would. If I was that worried about his past, I probably wouldn't be considering marrying him.

A: No, we should just wait and check out their character.

A: No, why would I marry someone that needed an STD check? Even if he had a past, I would want to be able to trust him.

Girls, are you so brilliant that you know the detailed sexual history of every person that previously came in contact with your future spouse? Even he doesn't always know. Wake up and start to protect yourself and maybe your future children.

Q: *Would you ever ask to see or pull a credit or business report on your soul mate?*

A: No, that would be devious.

A: No, financial status is not that important to me.

A: No, I don't care that much about money.

A: Any intelligent person with a brain can figure out how the other person is with money.

A: No, because I wouldn't like it if he did it to me.

A: No, it's none of my business.

A: No, if he's my soul mate, I can trust him.

A: If I had to check his credit, I'm not sure he'd really be my soul mate.

A: I shouldn't have to.

Girls! You'd better care about money because you will need to know that your husband can make it and use it wisely as a gift from God to provide for you and your children. Many good men and women with hearts of gold have difficulty handling the gold. Caring about money doesn't mean you are a gold digger. Quit worrying about how you look and check it out!

* * *

What these women are really saying is that:

(a) They are afraid they'd discover something unpleasant with which they'd have to deal.

(b) They are afraid that if they checked, their soul mate might get angry; they fear his rejection, anger, or worse—the end of the relationship over an argument.

(c) They are afraid to appear devious, calculating, or cold to their potential mate or others.

(d) They are afraid to appear insecure because they have developed a confident outward persona that the other one loves, and they risk rejection if they reveal their authentic self.

A true soul mate would want to give you every sense of security and would be mature enough to understand that full disclosure is not a threat, demand, or sign of insecurity. People who handle money might have past debt that loom over them or a history of credit card abuse. People who have been faithful to you before marriage may previously have been with others who were not. Verifying what you hear, see, suspect, or hope for is using the gifts God gave you.

Express Yourself

Finally, learn about others by sharing yourself. Let others know what you think and feel. Expressing yourself helps to reveal their character. You can't come to an ultimate conclusion about a soul mate by just listening, observing, and verifying facts. You have to open up and see how they respond to you.

I'll never forget my last date with Paul. I had my mental list of the things I wanted in a man. For the first few dates, I was careful not to reveal too much of myself, something I have tended to do too quickly in the past. I was practicing getting every bit of information about him I could.

Everything Paul said and did fit beautifully with my little list of the perfect man. After several dates, I actually got excited that this relationship could have some real potential . . . until I relaxed and began to express myself on the dance floor one night. We were at a charity dinner/dance for a homeless shelter, and the guests included many prominent people. Since I've lived in Palm Springs for over thirty years, I knew most of the guests and enjoyed mingling with the community leaders. The themed event featured a band that was playing lively country western hits. A local minister was caught up in the spirit of the evening and doing a cute little two-step alone. As Paul and I left the dance floor, I joined the minister, whom I've known for years, and we clowned around a little, laughing and carrying on like two kids. When the music was over, I returned to our table, where Paul sat stiffly like a titanic-sized iceberg in an Armani suit. A friend later told me Paul had commented on how ridiculous I looked goofing around on the dance floor, especially with a minister. Okay, I admit I didn't look very elegant in my expensive dress and heels doing a cowboy bit, but can't a girl have a little fun? I knew immediately that in simply being who I was, in expressing myself, Paul had revealed something about his character that I did not like. He dumped me shortly thereafter, which was fine with me. Can you imagine being married to someone who expects you to be Queen Elizabeth at every moment? No, thank you.

Some people are on their very best behavior before marriage, but after the wedding, watch out. Many singles are afraid to show their authentic self because they might be rejected. While dating, I think it's important to watch for signs and red flags in the other person, but it's just as critical to take off your own mask and be real. It helps you enjoy the relationship even more. And whether or not he or she ends up being your soul mate, it's less work and worry. It also speeds up the selection process by allowing the other person to decide if they really want you—warts and all. I'd rather be rejected on a dance floor than in a divorce court. Wouldn't you?

Testing the Theory

In our search for a soul mate, at some point we just have to let go and make up our mind one way or the other. In the Academy Award winning movie *A Beautiful Mind*, actor Russell Crowe portrayed John Forbes Nash, Jr., the Nobel Laureate mathematical genius. When Russell's character, John, is courting his college sweetheart, Alicia, he worries about making the final decision to marry her, thinking he might need more "empirical data" to see if she's really the one. John wants to be sure, as all prudent scientists do, but his alter ego reminds him that in love, no one is ever completely sure. We should take a lesson from the movie character and try to approach our L.O.V.E. equation with a balance of both cold, hard statistical facts and the equally important emotions and attraction we feel.

Recently, at a dinner party I met Tom, who shared a delightful story of how he decided to marry his wife, Marjorie. While he was in college, Tom worked nights delivering pizza. One evening he made a delivery to Margie's dorm, where she was working at the switchboard. They began to date and, like most of us, Tom was quietly assessing where his relationship with Margie might go. "I remember the exact night I fell in love with her," Tom told me. "It was only our third date, but she relaxed like she hadn't done before, and actually started acting a little silly." Tom is a soft-spoken and serious man, not one that would seem to tolerate silliness. But as he finished his story, his face softened. He got those bright eyes and sentimental smile that only long-time lovers have and added, "When Margie's cute, girlish self emerged, that's the minute I fell in love with her." Margie's light touch was exactly what young Tom had needed.

Who knows? If Tom had weighed only statistical facts in Margie's case, he may not have married her. But because of all the good things Tom observed—and how he felt when she expressed her real self with him—Margie married Tom Monaghan, who eventually went from pizza delivery boy to the founder of the billion dollar Domino's Pizza™ empire. Today Tom is planning to celebrate his fortieth wedding anniversary in the South of France with the soul mate whose sweet silliness won his heart.

.O.V.E. Is Not New

Learning to L.O.V.E. someone using your head as well as your heart is a smart way to ensure you make the wisest choice possible. Twinkie used her instincts and *listened* to the new people around her, *observed* their body language, *verified* by walking closer and sniffing, and then *expressed* herself, watching to see how others would accept or reject her. Only until she had taken these four steps, did she decide to crawl up in someone's lap.

Eliezer did the same thing. He *listened* to Rebekah and her family. He *observed* how Laban treated his sister and how the family interacted. He *verified* that she was indeed part of Abraham's kin, was available for marriage, and would have the blessings of her family. He continued to *express* his own observations, intentions, and desires, so he could see how Laban and Rebekah would respond to him.

Then he asked, "Whose daughter are you? Please tell me, is there room in your father's house for us to spend the night?"

She answered him, "I am the daughter of Bethuel, the son that Milcah bore to Nahor." And she added, "We have plenty of straw and fodder, as well as room for you to spend the night." Then the man bowed down and worshiped the Lord, saying, "Praise be to the Lord, the God of my master Abraham, who has not abandoned his kindness and faithfulness to my master. As for me, the Lord has led me on the journey to the house of my master's relatives."

The girl ran and told her mother's household about these things. Now Rebekah had a brother named Laban, and he hurried out to the man at the spring. As soon as he had seen the nose ring, and the bracelets on his sister's arms, and had heard Rebekah tell what the man said to her, he went out to the man and found him standing by the camels near the spring. "Come, you who are blessed by the Lord," he said. "Why are you standing out here? I have prepared the house and a place for the camels." So the man went to the house, and the camels were unloaded. Straw and fodder were brought for the camels, and water for him and his men to wash their feet. (Genesis 24:23–32)

Thousands of years ago a humble, but wise, servant made L.O.V.E. a part of his search for a soul mate and was successfully rewarded. Are you ready to L.O.V.E. someone?

What Does My Fear Say?

I'm afraid to really investigate or confirm what I think I see and hear. I want this to be the one. What if I find something bad?

What Does My Faith Say?

If I discover a problem with a potential soul mate, God has given me the means to work through it. This might mean letting them go and being alone again. God will lead me to love, and I can choose to trust God, even if I can't trust others.

What Should I Remember?

- *My false self and the "I wants" can get in the way of making a careful choice in soul mates.*
- *I won't always just know; I'll have to use my head as well as my heart.*
- *Making a good choice requires a lot more work than I ever thought.*

10

Step 7:
Be Willing to Wait

Without saying a word, the man watched her closely to learn whether or not the Lord had made his journey successful (Genesis 24:21).

Shana (pronounced SHAW-nuh) Graham is petite, slender, and has delicately chiseled features. Her big, blue eyes are set against ivory skin and framed by dark brown waves. When she laughs, her smile sparkles like the rhinestones in her beauty pageant tiara. You'd never guess that Shana, the reigning Mrs. California 2001, also is mother of four and wife to Robert, and she loves to ride motorcycles. When she was younger, after winning a racing competition, Shana delighted in hopping off her motorcycle at the judges stand, pulling off her helmet, shaking out her long wavy curls, and shocking the cheering crowd, who had assumed she was a boy.

I met Shana when she came to Upper CLASS to polish her public speaking presentations. As she shared the story of her life, I was particularly interested in her early dating experiences and her romance with Robert. At nineteen, Shana was about to go off to college but instead stayed home to be in a friend's wedding. At the church, she first saw Robert in a back pew and immediately knew he was "the one." Shana even remembers coming home after the wedding, kicking off her shoes, and jumping up on the bed to talk with her mother, telling her that she knew someday she would marry the man she'd seen in church that day. Shana never did leave town for college, and three months later she married Robert. As a young woman preparing for marriage, Shana thought she'd done all the right things: asked God for his blessings in her search for a husband, sought the counsel of her parents, looked only in good places, and asked the advice of friends and family. But Shana neglected one important step—waiting. Three months is hardly long enough to get to know anyone.

Shortly after the wedding, Shana and her new husband encountered terrible marriage problems that lasted over ten years. They fought, separated, reconciled, fought again, drained their finances, and exhausted their families. "It was a living hell on earth," Shana reflected. She told me it was only with mutual commitment to their vows,

God's grace, hard work, thousands of hours of counseling, help from friends, prayers, and nights of endless tears, that they made it through the tough times.

I asked Shana, if looking back, she had seen red flags. "No, I honestly didn't," she told me. "It's not that I ignored any big warnings. The problems that came up later were deeply hidden, and I was too naïve to know what to look for." I told Shana I understood because in my marriage I hadn't seen the signs either, but I admitted I did not wait long enough for any signs to appear. I asked her, "Shana, do you think maybe you would have seen some signs if you had waited more than three months to get married?"

Shana admitted that life would have been much different if she and Robert had set a date and then given themselves time to wait. She also admitted that her father had shared his uneasiness about their situation, but she ignored his concerns. "I realize I was basing my decisions on my emotions, and by ignoring my father's fears and not waiting a longer time to test the relationship, I only invited trouble." Thankfully, Shana and Robert are now determined to talk to and teach their own children about the right way to find a soul mate.

The Gift of Time

Couples who find themselves in trouble like Shana and Robert often divorce. If they stay together for the kids or for financial security, they endure a miserable marriage.

Some have affairs. In very few cases both partners work to overcome the root problems. And probably none of these couples realize that in their poor judgment, lack of advice, and most of all—failing to wait—that they might as well have picked out a divorce lawyer when they picked out their silver pattern.

In her book *The Starter Marriage,* author Pamela Paul describes the increasing trend of young people (Generation X) who commit to a lifelong marriage but find themselves divorced in three to five years or less. She says, "A starter marriage isn't a whim or a fantasy of a misbegotten affair— it's a real marriage between a man and a woman, bound together by love, personal beliefs, and, often, religious oath. A starter marriage doesn't feel like one when you're engaged or when you're inside it. It is charged with all the hope, expectations, and dreams that inspire almost all marriages. All starter marriages truly believe they are getting married forever."[1]

* * *

What's happening here? Obviously these couples who never make it to their fifth wedding anniversary are *not* doing it God's way. Their marriages fail quickly for many reasons, including these common factors:

- The husband and wife are not really "one adult man and one adult woman." At least one of them, if not both, are emotionally and spiritually stuck at about age ten (Mommy, this is too hard!) or maybe age thirteen (Mom's not gonna tell me what to do!).

- They lack the emotional maturity to stick to a commitment or to do the hard work necessary to make a relationship last, because they've rarely been held accountable to follow through on anything.
- The couple has no family or social teaching, pressure, or support, to go the distance.
- Both partners may hold college degrees, but they lack communication, financial, or other relationship skills.
- They saw the red flags and ignored them, resulting in failure before they began.
- They rushed into the relationship, not holding back emotionally or sexually until time could reveal the red flags.

*H*ow People Handle Waiting Differently

Waiting, especially when you feel like you're falling in love, can be a challenge to some people. It often depends on your natural personality blend whether you'll welcome waiting, or bristle at the very thought. The extroverted Popular Sanguine and Powerful Choleric temperaments usually don't like to wait for anything. With their higher energy level, they are more prone to pushing than patience. The two introverted temperaments, Perfect Melancholy and Peaceful Phlegmatic, naturally, find it much easier to slow down and carefully consider life. While the extroverts (which we also know to be the classic Type A personalities) could learn a thing or two about waiting from the introverts, the Type B's sometimes wait too long, settling into "analysis paralysis." They're actually too worried about making the right decision, so they stay stuck in indecision or procrastination. Can you relate to any of these personality patterns?

Sanguines: The *popular* people like things light, easy, and fun. In their natural childlike sweetness and energy, they also can be childish in wanting it all and wanting it now. They are used to charming everyone into getting what they want. They hate to wait and will open their mouth and let you know just how much they hate it!

Cholerics: The *powerful*, driven personalities hate to wait because they like to keep producing, working, moving, growing, and pushing ahead. They thrive on the long mental list of all the things they accomplish each day. Rarely stopping to enjoy the process, they keep their focus just far enough ahead to miss what's right in front of them. Wait? What's useful or productive about that?

Melancholy: The *perfect* personalities care deeply about everything and especially in finding the perfect partner. They are usually most meticulous in their decision making, worried that they haven't considered enough facts or waited long enough. They can fret, stew, and even obsess about their soul mate. They have no trouble waiting, but they eventually will need to make up their mind.

Phlegmatic: The *peaceful* people have the quietest strength; they are easygoing, kind, loving, adaptable, and most of all, they prefer to wait. Waiting and watching comes naturally to them. They wait, and if there is no loud Choleric leader or sassy Sanguine to push them, they will wait forever. However, Phlegmatics especially avoid conflict, trouble, or bad news. While they have no trouble waiting, they might wait with blinders on or their head in the sand.

Usually you're born with one or a blend of two of these temperaments, since the other two are natural opposites. Although one or two personality patterns will govern your initial and primary response, some have developed attitudes of all the temperaments. Whatever your natural tendency toward waiting is, you need to begin to understand why you have trouble taking the time, and making the time, to be smart about your search for a soul mate. Learning to wait and maximizing your time is a skill you will need for any successful relationship.

Why We Hate to Wait

Even though everyone deals differently with waiting, all of us share some universal reasons we hate to wait. In preparing yourself for a soul mate, I think you need to

take a look at why you struggle with waiting and seek outside help in those areas. Common reasons for rushing
through relationships include:

We hate to wait because we are emotionally starved.
Have you ever gone grocery shopping when you're starving? If you're like me, you buy more food than you need
for the week and make poor choices because it all looks
good. When your stomach is growling, you're tired, or
overworked, you can feel deprived, and you may even eat
half the bag of cookies before you get to the checkout
counter. Relationships are the same way. When you're not
getting enough healthy companionship, love, emotional
support, friendship, encouragement, and social activity,
you'll be much more prone to jump into a relationship
that is too much for you, not healthy, or you'll start
devouring what does not yet belong to you.

One blunt baby boomer told me, "Had I followed my
gut instinct, I would have kissed her good-bye after three
dates. Why did I stay? Honestly? I was desperately lonely
and wanted sex. I feel like a whore." People of all ages and
personalities tend to pursue sexual pleasures to ease their
relational pain, to reward themselves, to feel good, and to
fill the emotional and spiritual emptiness.

To be able to wait in your search and assessment of a
possible soul mate, you need to meet your needs in as
many areas as possible. That means plenty of personal
interaction, fellowship, and healthy hugging and touching

with friends, family, children, and other loved ones. To be able to say no, singles should not stay isolated or alone too long.

We hate to wait because we have little else that satisfies us. Most divorcees that I counsel admit that they had unrealistic expectations that their spouse would meet all their emotional, mental, social, spiritual, physical, and financial needs. When they were babies, Mom and Dad did meet all those needs. During childhood, when they were bored, Mom came up with activities. When they needed help, Dad saved the day. But as single adults, if they haven't learned to meet their own needs in healthy ways, they'll be looking for a soul mate who replaces Mommy or Daddy. It's a losing situation from the start: they subconsciously want a parent, but they don't want to be married to a parent.

If you can't wait for a soul mate, then you probably haven't cultivated a wide variety of other satisfying interests. Cook up a rich, interesting life for yourself, which will bring you immediate joy, instead of looking for some unknown person who may or may not arrive. I admit that pets, hobbies, work, trips, and companions can't always be as satisfying as a true soul mate, but I consider them to be delicious appetizers. If the main course is delayed, or never arrives, I can fill up quite nicely on life's hors d'oeuvres.

We hate to wait because we think it will never come again. It's easy to see now that the emotional responses we developed as children stay with us into adulthood. When

I was young, I often fell into depression the day after Christmas and the day after my birthday. Those days were built up for so long and were so fabulously festive and fantastic that the day after was a major letdown. Waiting a whole year seemed like a lifetime. As far as I felt, it was over forever. It's almost like it would never come again. That's normal for kids, but for adults it's almost ridiculous. Grownups can wait another year because they have lived long enough to know that fun times keep coming back around. If you're depressed by the thought that you'll never find your soul mate, or you'll never have love like this again, perhaps all you need is to live long enough to know that love keeps coming back around.

We hate to wait because we have a distorted view of time. If you could draw "eternity" across the length of a piece of 8½ × 11 inch paper, it would be a line that spanned the eleven inches and also extended off the desk, out the front door, into the next county, and beyond. Now stop to think that your lifetime is less than one-eighth of an inch on that miles-long line. You stress and cry because you might not get the love you want in this short lifetime, but you forget your belief in eternity and a loving God who promises sparkling joy, perfect happiness, and endless love—all the way into the next county and beyond. Are you willing to wait for that?

We hate to wait because we have microwave mentality. I love to cook, but as a single I admit to being the microwave queen. (Did you know that the microwave supposedly was invented after a researcher walked by a radar tube and a chocolate bar in his pocket melted?) More than once I've opened the freezer, pulled out two Lean Cuisines, thought they both looked good but chose the one that cooked in only five minutes instead of seven because it was faster. I'm pathetic! Just this week I upgraded my computer with a CD burner and an additional memory card so it would be faster. (I can hardly tell the difference.) I'm still behind. This whole rush-rush-rush thing is like one of Stephen King's mysterious life forces threatening to take over the world! In a front-page article in August 2001, *USA Today* writer Bruce Horovitz described the nation's unofficial, new motto—"Humming Along Like a Timex on No-Doz: 24/7." Horovitz detailed what he calls a cultural earthquake, where stores and businesses increasingly are staying open day and night so we, the consumer, can get what we want when we want it with no waiting. He quotes David Shi, cultural guru and president of Furman University, "The level of impatience in American culture is almost pathological. We grow impatient when other aspects of our lives don't match the immediacy of the computer— even if it's just a pizza craving at 3:00 a.m."[2]

One of the reasons we don't wait to let time reveal a potential soul mate's character is because we have that microwave mentality. We want to find someone yummy, quickly scan their calorie content, pop them in the oven, and get married. But you only have to look at the divorce rates to know that what's good for soufflés is not good for soul mates!

What's So Great about Waiting?

Waiting develops patience. Patience is a virtue that you can, and should, use over and over in all your relationships. If you want people to be patient with you, you need to develop patience for others.

Waiting allows God to keep working on your soul mate. Maybe he or she isn't ready for you yet. If you knew that meeting your soul mate was right around the corner, and God needed a little more time to gift you with the perfect present, would you be willing to wait?

Waiting gives you more time to work on yourself. Remember the more mature, well-balanced, and emotionally healthy you become, the higher caliber soul mate you will attract.

Waiting develops stronger emotional muscles. Do you remember as a child being stuck in the car on a long trip with your family and you had to go to the bathroom? What did Mom and Dad tell you? "Just hold it until we stop." We wiggled and squirmed and whined a little louder, but we learned to hold it. As a result, our little muscles grew stronger as we trained them to delay what they naturally felt like doing. When you're dating, you think you need to give in to other natural impulses, but you need to "hold it." I call it emotional potty training!

Waiting allows you to see and test quality before making long-term commitment. My twenty-something nephew, Chris, started working for a company but was on probation until his employer could see what strengths and weaknesses he brought to the firm. He wasn't eligible for insurance, vacation, or other perks until the company decided he was worth their investment. He didn't like the policy at first, but later was glad he wasn't hired permanently because he decided to quit and sign up for the Army instead. The recruiting officers hired him right away, gave him a permanent commitment, and a $5,000 advance. But guess what? In the military, men and women must still go through intense screening and training over time until they are assigned to their final duties and location. In boot camp Chris learned how to wait, something he'll also have to do when he looks for his soul mate. Waiting will help you make wise choices based on the strengths and weaknesses you see over time.

Waiting helps to keep you safe. I've been driving for over thirty years, but in the last few years I've never seen so many people ignore red lights. There've been times, after the light has turned green, I've had to wait for five or six cars coming from the opposite direction to turn left in front of me, none of whom seemed to even care that I might hit them. They wanted to go where they wanted, when they wanted, and I had better stay out of their way! I've even gotten dirty looks as I tried to go forward. Our local sheriff confirmed that the majority of accidents occur when the lights turn green and we assume the coast is clear. We're supposed to wait at green lights until it is safe to proceed. Waiting, even for soul mates, can help keep us safe from being hurt in many ways.

Waiting allows time to reveal truth. When I was a Girl Scout in the 1960s, I sold marigold flower seeds door-to-door to raise money for summer camp. Back then, for only a nickel, you could get pale yellow, gold, orange, or even red, but you wouldn't know their color until they bloomed. My sister and I would guess, hope, and even bet our allowance on the color, but no amount of speculation or observation would reveal what we'd gotten. We had to wait. I've seen this principle proven time and time again in relationships. The longer you spend getting to know someone, the closer you'll be to knowing his or her real character. Waiting helps you see someone's true colors.

Waiting can get you the best deal of all. I love the original cherry-almond smell of Jergen's hand and body lotion, but it only goes on sale at Walgreen's about once every three months, which is a long time for me to wait. I can buy it whenever I want for a ridiculously high price, or I can wait and get the two-for-one price. The impulse to spend can be a lot like the impulse to find a soul mate; you can pay a really high price if you're not prudent. Waiting for the right time and the right person can get you the best deal with the lowest price.

Waiting can reap unexpected rewards. When I was little, I learned many lessons about waiting. As the oldest of eight children, I was expected to wait until all my younger siblings had their turn or made their choice. When I did, Mom and Dad often would give me something extra for waiting. This attitude still pays off when I am waiting in line at the bank, grocery store, or the cosmetics counter at Nordstrom's. Clerks appreciate a patient person, and because I'm willing to wait and not complain, push, or pout, I usually get the extra discount, the free video rental, or a full-sized lipstick as a reward. I think God also appreciates when one waits for a soul mate and will reward that patience. Regardless, waiting can be its own reward.

Waiting allows you to love others. Facing an unexpected delay gives those of us who are over-scheduled extra time to enjoy life. The other day at McDonald's I ended up in the longest line, of course, where I wanted to holler out so the whole place could hear, "Well, so much for FAST FOOD!" Instead, I recognized my bad attitude, took a deep breath, and looked around. I've decided that if God gives me extra time, I should use it to see who might need some love, encouragement, or a smile. I talked to the crabby old man standing behind me and got him to laugh at my joke. I helped a mother get ketchup while she held her baby, cola, and fries. I told the teenager in front of me that I liked his leopard-spotted hair. I really did; it was an amazing form of art! And like most teens, he probably needed to hear some encouraging words from an adult. I used my waiting to practice loving others. If you haven't found your soul mate, or are still wondering if he or she is the one, you can use this time to enjoy the rest of life and to love others. Waiting can be a gift.

How Long Should You Wait?

Since each of us is unique, every couple's timetable will be differ slightly, but here are some good rules of thumb:

- *You should wait* to move to deeper levels of mental, emotional, and spiritual intimacy until enough time has passed to reveal their character and intentions, and your response to them.
- *You should wait* until after a few dates before you put a potential mate on the "hot seat" with your stated intentions, list of qualities, and questions. But you can start L.O.V.E. on the first date with, "Tell me about your family . . ."
- *You should wait* at least one year before you make a final commitment to marriage. A year takes you through a normal family cycle of holidays, work, anniversaries,

and other time periods that help to reveal a person's character.

- *You should wait* if you've just ended a long-term relationship or marriage, at least a few years to do the work of stabilizing, grieving, healing, and regaining your emotional balance.
- *You should wait* to become sexually intimate until you have the fullest protection and commitment on every level, and that means only legal marriage as God intended.

Yes, it's hard to do, and no, it's not impossible or old fashioned. Ask Rene Russo, the glamorous Hollywood actress who asked her fiancé to respect her purity until they were married. He did because he truly loved her.

* * *

No time period can ever reveal the whole person. Every newly married couple will continue to discover new things about one another over time. That's life. But to reduce the risk of having your heart broken, be willing to wait and make good use of the time you share.

What about waiting too long? If you're prone to procrastination or afraid of failing, you might wait too long. Waiting too long can create tension and cause fear, doubt, and resentment for one or both parties. Waiting too long also tempts you to start living together or enjoying the emotional and sexual intimacy that God created for a committed husband and wife.

Waiting to have sexual and full emotional intimacy until after marriage is an absolute must for anyone who wants to protect themselves, the other person, and their families. Waiting for marriage is how God designed sex to work best, and history shows the damage that sleeping and living together without marriage has done to homes, families, and society. The National Marriage Project at Rutgers University (September 1999) reports that living together is *not* marriage friendly. The study found that cohabiting couples are 48 percent more likely to divorce than those who aren't.[3] Other findings show these couples are less happy and suffer more domestic violence, and that most of them break up within three years. They then take their unhealed hearts and unhealthy habits into the next relationship. So much for their version of love.

God asks us to wait—just awhile—to get the very best out of the gifts he gave man and woman. Isaac waited, Rebekah waited, and Eliezer waited. Different waiting for different reasons, but each with a happy ending.

Eliezer's Payoff

Even though Eliezer had already received his "sign," he didn't rush into anything but waited to see if Rebekah was what she appeared to be. Anyone can put on a smile and offer to do something nice for us, but what happens when it gets hard? Will they stop trying to please us and do a minimal job? Will they quit halfway through with some excuse? Will they complete the task but whine the whole time? Eliezer wanted to see if Rebekah would carry through, even when it took longer than she expected; even if it was harder (and the camels were meaner) than she'd anticipated. He waited to see if she would keep her cheerful countenance the whole time or if she'd regret her offer. Eliezer knew that what a person says can be completely different than what he or she does. When Rebekah passed the test, Abraham's servant still *waited* to meet the family and *waited* for the right time to take her back home.

In a committed relationship, you want a soul mate who will not back out after a few years of marriage when the going gets tough. Anyone can fall in love with you, adore your little quirks, and promise to be true forever. But you want someone who will actually do whatever it takes to get the job done without complaining or quitting halfway through. You want someone who, when the going gets tough, will even take that bullet for you. The only way you can tell if someone has that level of maturity is to *wait* and watch over time to see how they handle other difficult parts of life. You need to *wait* for signs, *wait* to watch the family and friends, and *wait* for the right time.

The Apostle Paul wrote a beautiful description of love that people of all faiths have cherished for centuries. In 1 Corinthians 13:4 he starts with, "Love is patient . . . . "

Are you?

What Does My Fear Say?

I'm afraid I can't wait that long. It seems unnatural to have to hold off so long for something that is so good or beautiful. What if I lose him or her?

What Does My Faith Say?

God promises to give me the gifts and the grace to wait and to develop a relationship the best way for both of us. I can look forward to a long life of true love if I'm willing to wait for the very best.

What Should I Remember?

- *Sex* blinds you *and* binds you *so* you *can't see what you're stuck with until it's too late.*
- *Waiting is never forever.*
- *You wait for other good things, why not a soul mate?*

11

Step 8:
Save Your Best for Last

When Kristin met Eric, she jumped onto the same old dating merry-go-round many singles have ridden: you date a few times, talk and have a great time, start to consider yourselves boyfriend and girlfriend, and then end up in bed. It feels romantic, sexy, and fun, which is the way God intended it for husband and wife. But without the protection and commitment of the marriage covenant, you keep going 'round and 'round and 'round until you get sick and one of you hollers, "Stop!" But by then, it's too late. Someone has been hurt.

Kristin gave everything she had to Eric because she loved him and ignored the little voice in her head that said, "What about commitment?" She knew (or thought she knew) that the quickest way to scare off a man was to bring up the "C" word. She spent almost every night at Eric's place—cooking his dinner, giving his house a woman's touch, and even doing his laundry. She took care of his kids, bought them birthday presents when Eric forgot, shared her paycheck, and helped him in his ongoing court battles with his ex-wife. Although she sometimes felt like Eric's wife, there was no ring on her finger. After a few years, she finally admitted that Eric was getting everything he wanted from her with no strings attached; he was getting all the benefits of a wife with none of the responsibilities. Kristin, however, was giving everything and getting none of the legal, financial, physical, or emotional protection and provision that a husband is meant to provide. She felt insecure and anxious. Finally she pressured Eric into an engagement ring. The next step was setting a wedding date, but when Eric refused, they broke up.

"It wasn't so much about sex, although I see now why it was wrong," Kristin told me. "What really hurt was the whole 'wife' role I was playing that was too much too soon. With his kids, and our friends, families, and neighbors, we were a couple, but we really weren't. I gave him everything without limits, and he spooned his love out to me in carefully measured cupfuls."

Kristin has since recognized the need for emotional purity and abstinence of the heart. "I thought God's way was keeping us from having any fun, but now I see it's to protect our hearts and souls." After Kristin told me this story, we reflected on how all little children think their parents' rules are intended to keep them from having a good time. It's not until they mature that they understand the reason for the rules is to protect them and give them the very best of what life has to offer.

Kristin finally decided to do it God's way. After she and Eric broke up, Kristin spent a morning clearing out all the remnants of her life with him. As she quietly sobbed, she stopped to stare at her diamond engagement ring. The sparkles of love were replaced by a dull ache, and the gold band seemed to be nothing more than the cheap brass carousel ring, reminding her of the painful ups and downs of their relationship.

Kristin decided to write a letter, and afterward she wrapped the ring up in the stationery. The next morning, she anonymously placed it in the church collection basket. The note read:

Dear God,

I'm giving this ring back to You, along with all the shame and hurt and anger I feel. I trust that in Your time You will bring me a husband, and until then You will provide for all my needs.

Your Daughter, Kristin

ebekah's Ring

"Then I put the ring on her nose and the bracelets on her arms, and I bowed down and worshiped the Lord. I praised

*the Lord, the God of my master Abraham, who had led
me on the right road to get the granddaughter of my master's brother for his son. Now if you will show kindness
and faithfulness to my master, tell me; and if not, tell me,
so I may know which way to turn."*

*Laban and Bethuel answered, "This is from the Lord;
we can say nothing to you one way or the other. Here is
Rebekah; take her and go, and let her become the wife of
your master's son, as the Lord has directed."*

*When Abraham's servant heard what they said, he
bowed down to the ground before the Lord. Then the servant brought out gold and silver jewelry and articles of
clothing and gave them to Rebekah; he also gave costly
gifts to her brother and to her mother. Then he and the
men who were with him ate and drank and spent the night
there.* (Genesis 24:47–54)

Rebekah's ring was worth much more than Kristin's
because it was backed by purity, promise, and protection.
At the well, Eliezer had given Rebekah a ring, but no more
than that until the full commitment had been made.
Although he felt sure that Rebekah was "the one," he nev-
ertheless waited, watched, and went through the proper
procedures before giving her all the gifts he'd carefully prepared. He saved the very best until last.

Two principles from this story can help us see how to
handle the gifts God has entrusted to us:

(1) Eliezer valued the treasures his master had given him. He did not want to give them away until he'd confirmed his decision . . . and the final commitment had been given and received.

Do you value, much less understand, what God has entrusted to you? Some of God's gifts are designed and meant to be shared only with your soul mate—in the context of total giving that occurs with the lifelong commitment of marriage. Your mind, heart, and body are the most precious presents that you bring to a marriage relationship. You also bring your family, (and sometimes your children from previous relationships), your friends, your skills, and your physical and financial assets. To give any of these away too soon, or too fully, to someone who has not yet earned your trust or committed himself or herself to you can leave you broken and bitter, and can hurt others as well. Although you're familiar with sexual abstinence until marriage, you might not realize that you often give too much too soon of *other* parts of yourself that cause even deeper pain when and if you break up.

(2) Eliezer gave some small gifts to Rebekah only after he'd watched her long enough to know she probably was going to be Isaac's bride.

As soon as Rebekah had completed her task of watering the camels, showing to be true to her word, Eliezer wanted her to know he was serious about looking for a wife for his master's son and wanted to share a little of the treasure he had for her. He gave her a ring and bracelets. She could now see he meant business; everyone else in town (including all the men) also knew that Eliezer meant business. Engagement rings are meant to keep the wolves away!

This part of the story teaches that when you're dating, or courting a potential spouse, you can and should begin to share a little of yourself on every level, to let the other person know you desire them. Holding back too much and refusing to let another person into your heart is the opposite extreme of giving too much too soon and can keep you from developing true intimacy. The giving process is a delicate balance and takes wisdom, practice, and grace, but you still can save the best for last. Like Eliezer, even though you begin to give of yourself and the gifts God has given you, you still should continue the investigative process until both parties are completely satisfied with the courtship, and the commitment has been made.

Intimacy

Intimacy is more than just sexual closeness; it covers all areas of being human. Intimacy can be sharing, relating, coupling, and bonding on various levels. The more you share, the deeper the bond. The deeper the bond, the more you hurt if the relationship fails. There are other areas of intimacy that need to be saved, as you save the best for last:

- *Mental intimacy* is a deep sharing of thoughts, ideas, conversations, ideologies, and beliefs. This occurs in long conversations and exchanges that bring you in closer agreement or intellectual understanding. When I dated dashing Jean-Pierre, we shared some delicious dinners and deep conversations about the world, politics, religion, history, and other chewy subjects. I relished our stimulating mental bonding along with his hearty laugh. But after several months, when it was clear he did not want to pursue me any longer, I found the end to our relationship hurt even more because of the intellectual intimacy we'd shared and lost.

- *Emotional intimacy* is revealing your inner fears, hopes, dreams, and desires. This happens when you're willing to expose your weak side, share common visions, and provide emotional support and help for one another. Tom poured out all his troubles to his neighbor Karen, who listened sweetly and offered help. She helped him reconcile with his estranged father and spent months caring for his daughter after school. But when Karen married Armando, Tom was crushed. Tom had hoped for a romance with Karen. Although they had not been physically intimate, part of Tom's heart went with Karen when she left because of the emotional intimacy they'd developed.

- *Financial intimacy* is sharing your money, supporting, or paying for another. It can be an act of bonding, especially when you put someone else on your charge accounts, agree to pay for their living expenses, or loan them money. Jeff felt sorry for his girlfriend, Lisa, who'd been on welfare, so he bought a house and let her live in it rent-free. Then he paid for her daughter's private school tuition and even bought her a new van. Lisa and her kids were even on Jeff's Blockbuster video rental account. When they broke up, Lisa told everyone that Jeff kicked her out, her children left him nasty phone messages, and they ran up charges on his credit card. Jeff realized it wasn't just about sex; he'd shared too much, too soon in financial areas that should have been saved for marriage.

- *Social intimacy* is spending time at each other's homes, with each other's families, meeting the kids, the parents, and the friends. Any activity that families typically do together, such as grocery shopping, yard work, or house decorating, can create a deep social bond. Renee spent several nights a week cooking dinner for Bill and his friends. On weekends they worked in Bill's yard, where Renee planted a vegetable garden. Renee was quick to make friends with Bill's family and all his neighbors. She cried bitter tears when they broke up because she'd bonded socially, not only with Bill, but with many others in his life. She'd probably never see any of them, or her tomatoes, again.

- *Spiritual intimacy* is sharing prayer time or acts of worship, especially in community. Worshiping God together can be powerful when two people are alone. Sharing spiritual activity binds you to the congregation with whom you're singing, communing, or praying. This communion with God and others goes right to your very heart and, if you lose it, the pain can be devastating. A unique spark is created when a man and woman worship together as a couple before God. Many couples who dated "safely" by going to services together have told me that the closest they ever felt was standing next to each other in the pews. When they broke up, the tearing of the spiritual bond hurt as much as anything else. Time in church together sounds smart, but depending on when you start, it can make you feel married too soon.

Intimacy on all levels is normal and necessary to create and sustain relationships, but the deeper you bond, the deeper you hurt (and hurt others) if the relationship ends. In dating, you should be willing to wait and watch the other person's character reveal itself before you meet the family, introduce your children, or spend close time at each other's homes.

Common Myths about Sex Before Marriage

Like Kristin and Eric, we all grow up seeing either our parents, relatives, or the people on television in a loving relationship, and we naturally want it for ourselves. Even if

they didn't grow up in a loving home, most women especially are quick to play house by giving their whole self to
a man from the very beginning. If playing house means
they get sex without responsibility or commitment, guys
will go for it too. Singles have been tricked and trapped.
They've bought into so many myths they can't see the red
flags anymore. Here are some common lies:

Sex outside marriage is okay if it's "safe." If you define
"safe" as not getting pregnant and not contracting disease,
you're still not right. Medical experts have confirmed that
the *only* safe sex is abstinence. Sex outside marriage also
can hurt the mind, bruise the tender emotions, and wound
the spirit. Where's the safety in that?

*I need to know if we're sexually compatible before I
make a commitment.* Almost anyone can be sexually compatible. If you let go of false expectations, and fill your
heart with genuine caring, then nature does the rest. The
same hormone (oxytocin) that bonds a mother to her baby
when she breast feeds is released with sexual activity and
helps to powerfully bond the couple. Mothers aren't
always naturally compatible with their babies, but with
time, love, and hormones, it happens. Men and women,
alike, need to understand that sexual satisfaction can be
as emotionally critical to a man as security and support
are to a woman. Sex is important to both, but the desire
to test compatibility is more often an excuse for the man
to get the woman into bed.

God made us sexual; He is compassionate, so He'll understand if I have sex. God made you to eat, too, but gluttony is the sin of eating too much, and it's wrong to steal another's food. Just because you were made to eat doesn't mean you can eat what you want, when you want, without any consequences. Although your natural tendency is to give in to your cravings, you're commanded to have control over your appetites, not vice versa.

If I give him sex now, he will give me commitment later. I believe that women have to shoulder a large part of the responsibility for the increasing fatherless homes in America. We keep giving our bodies without commitment, hoping the man will eventually give in. It's an old dilemma: why should he "pay" with protection and commitment when he can get it for free?

Sex is a powerful urge; how can anyone expect me to control it? Anger's powerful, too, but if you act on it, you can hurt others or end up in jail. Society expects you and me to control our anger, our spending, our driving, our drinking, and other parts of our life. There are thousands of rules and regulations to keep us from hurting others (and ourselves), but few laws help us control our sexual urges. Without external restrictions we especially need self-control—a virtue we expect in others but often refuse to master for ourselves.

Using forms of protection is responsible sexual behavior. Consider this scenario. Barb expects her teenage son,

Joe, to be honest and stay out of the cash register when he works at Burger King. But Barb, as a concerned mother, presses a twenty dollar bill in his hand and says, "Joe, in case you do choose to steal, keep this $20 for protection so you can put it back in the register just in case anything might be missing." Barb just told her son she does not trust him to be either responsible or moral. She also gave him permission to cover himself and be even more dishonest if he got caught. Barb should tell her son that she expects him to be honest. If he steals, she will still love him but she will not bail him out. She'll stand back and give him the opportunity to learn from his mistake and handle the consequences like a man. Being fired or having difficulty getting a new job is all part of Joe's being responsible for his choice.

Responsible behavior is choosing morally, and fully accepting any consequences of that choice. If the consequence of unmarried sex is pregnancy, then the individual needs to become a responsible parent or give the baby up for adoption. Abortion currently may be a legal right, but it is totally wrong and grossly irresponsible.

It's both a man and a woman's responsibility to guard each other's hearts from pain, each other's bodies from disease, each other's minds from anxieties and fears, and each other's spirits from feeling separation from God. Sex outside marriage, as you'll read later, sets up both man and woman for so much potential pain and negative consequences that sex outside marriage can never be called "responsible."

Starving the Soul, Feeding the Heart

Laura Vanderkam, a recent Princeton graduate, entitled her newspaper article about modern college dating habits, "Hookups Starve the Soul." The editorial described the current phenomenon (hooking up) of young men and women getting together with the sole intention of physical or sexual intimacy with no expectations in the morning.[1] I had to laugh when I saw the updated phrase because every generation wants to give a new name to an old sin.

The Old Testament says that as far as human nature is concerned, "there is nothing new under the sun."[2] What today's young people calls hookups, my generation called a "one-night stand." Because I was curious to know what previous generations labeled short-term lust, I called my ninety-two year-old father, whose body is now weak but whose mind is still strong. I almost cried when I listened to his rattled old voice tell me, "Rosie, it's not that I can't remember what we called it, we just didn't talk openly or casually about it. Sleeping around is as old as time, but up until about the 1930s there was a graciousness in society such that raw things were not talked about, even among men. We were expected to be ladies and gentlemen. It may seem hypocritical, but there was a grace back then that's gone today."

Dad recalled that after the Great Depression over 13,000 banks went bankrupt, the unemployment rate was up over 20 percent, and thousands committed suicide. He said that people were sick of down times. Like a rubber band that's been pulled too tightly, society shot back in the 1930s with rising skirt hems, easy-access liquor, and a much more liberal attitude. Screen idols kissed on the lips, causing scandal everywhere. "The liberal trend accelerated in the late 1950s and 1960s with talk of free love, abortion, and divorce on demand," Dad told me sadly, and with the feeblest trace of old outrage.

"I know, Dad, I was there," I reminded him.

It never will matter what label we give to intimacy outside its proper place; it will always bring some form of permanent hurt to others. True love is patient, kind, and self-sacrificing. Sex is not love. Sex without the fullest giving of the marriage commitment may temporarily satisfy, but ultimately it starves the soul. Sex within the protection and full giving of marriage brings the best of all God's gifts to both people and feeds our hearts.

Even though human failing will always be with us, I hope we can get back to calling it what it is. As you read the list of what can happen when sex occurs outside marriage, you'll see that even the term "making love" is anything *but* love.

* * *

101 REASONS TO SAVE YOUR BEST FOR LAST

Sex outside marriage can develop these emotional consequences:

1. Fear of not being fully loved because there is no commitment

2. Anxiety about when or if commitment will happen

3. Anxiety about the other person pressuring you into commitment

4. Constant or recurring doubts about the other person's level of commitment

5. Bitterness toward the other person for not being willing to commit

6. Bitterness toward the other person for pressuring commitment

7. Fear of being discovered by parents, friends, or others

8. Fear of disapproval by family, friends, the church, God, or others

9. Preoccupation or even obsession with the relationship

10. Focusing too much on sex to keep the relationship going

11. Compromising your values to get sex or love

12. Shame or guilt at having to hide or keep secrets

13. Shame or guilt at lowering your standards, compromising

14. Shame or guilt at compromising the other person's values

15. Avoidance and denial of certain issues to maintain the sexual relationship

16. Stuffing feelings, dreams, and desires to maintain the sexual relationship

17. Developing permanent negative emotional patterns because you're locked in sexually

18. Fear of lies being uncovered and having to tell more lies

19. Feeling trapped or powerless

20. Fear of pregnancy

21. Fear of sexually transmitted diseases

22. Fear of rejection if you have a baby

23. Fear of parenthood and its responsibilities

24. Fear of being tied down to the wrong person through sexual behaviors

25. Fear of being abandoned or of breaking up

26. Fear of the shame and loneliness when you do break up

27. Anger at knowing the other person could walk out anytime

28. Using sex to control another person or to keep them around

29. Using sex to fit in and avoid rejection in social groups

30. Learning to disassociate feelings and inner intuition and conscience

31. Learning to walk on eggshells around the other person in hopes they will commit to you

32. Developing deep regret

33. Feeling cheap or dirty

34. Turning off your sensitivities to your partner's whole-person needs

35. Numbing your conscience and asking the other person to numb theirs

36. Developing manipulation skills to stay in a sexual relationship

37. Leading the other person into a relationship that will hurt them emotionally

38. Anger at the other person for not giving 100 percent

39. Anger at yourself for settling for less than you need or want

40. Anger at knowing you have no legal rights in the relationship

41. Anger at losing your dream of marriage or commitment

42. Shame or guilt at knowing you should be doing it another way

43. Frustration because the other person refuses to talk about commitment

44. Feeling hurt with no right to ask for what you need

45. Feeling jealous of others

46. Suffering mild or severe forms of depression

47. Losing hope that lifelong commitment and fidelity still exists

48. Losing hope that you can ever have a lifelong commitment with anyone

49. Loss of hope that you could find anyone who would not ridicule your wish for abstinence

50. Loss of respect for your partner since they don't listen to their conscience either

51. Loss of respect for your partner because they have such low self-control

52. Loss of trust that your partner will remain faithful and committed

Sex outside marriage involves these medical, emotional, and physical risks:

53. Suffering the physical pain and embarrassment of STDs (sexually transmitted diseases)

54. Falling into depression and requiring counseling and/or medication

55. Having to pay medical bills for ongoing diseases

56. Resorting to secrets and lies to hide your diseases

57. Possible infertility and related medical bills as a result of STDs

58. Losing the dream of ever having children because of STDs

59. Lowering your chances of future marriage because you can't have children

60. Possibility of giving STDs to your future husband or wife

61. Possible birth defects in your babies due to STDs

62. Suffering shame, guilt, anger, and anxiety over harming your children

63. Exposing yourselves to having to face the decision to abort

64. Dealing with fear, anger, guilt, costs, and other effects of abortion

65. Increased counseling costs as a result of post-abortion depression

66. Fear of being rejected by others because you choose life for your baby

67. Getting pregnant and being abandoned

68. Suffering from Post-Abortion Syndrome

69. Feeling ashamed at being an unwed mother or father

70. Losing the dream of being a family when your baby comes

71. Bringing your child into a broken family situation

72. Bearing the burden of being a single parent

73. Being socially isolated

74. Struggling with little or no emotional or financial support

75. Possibly having to spend thousands of dollars in court to get custody or support

76. Future difficulties of blending families and step-parents

77. Ongoing battles about weekend visitations

Sex outside marriage can bring these harmful elements into new marriage:

78. Fear or anxiety of repeated rejection
79. Inability to relax with or trust a new partner
80. Permanent mental images of previous partners, which affect your sexual responses
81. Worrying or wondering about your spouse's intimate or sensual memories of another
82. Conscious or subconscious comparison of your new partner with the old
83. Developing a criticism of your new partner based on what the old partner did
84. Bringing worry to your new partner that you still have the old one in your mind
85. Bringing worry to your new partner that they won't measure up like the others
86. Bringing perverted, distorted, or unhealthy sexual patterns to your marriage
87. Possibility of sexual dysfunction from previous emotional issues
88. Greatly increasing your chance of divorce

Sex outside marriage can result in these spiritual consequences:

89. Feeling far away from or unloved by God
90. A sense of failure, guilt, or shame before God
91. Twisting Scripture or other spiritual teachings to justify your actions

92. Staying away from church community out of fear or shame

93. Deciding to stop seeking God because he doesn't understand

94. Stunted spiritual maturity

95. Recurring dreams or nightmares

96. A lessened sensitivity to spiritual things

97. A distaste for conversation about spiritual matters

98. An uneasy feeling or anger about hearing truth

99. A disintegration of your body and mind from your spirit

100. Developing addictions that keep you from focusing on God

101. Lack of spiritual peace

You can see that saving the best for last is not a restriction on your freedoms, but a smart choice for getting the most out of life and love. You need to *grow up*, *slow down*, *hold off*, and *stay on* course to reap the endless benefits of dating, courtship, romance, sex, and marriage God's way.

* * *

Sex saved for marriage (God's way) results in:

1. Having enough time to learn about the other person without being hormonally blinded

2. Giving the other person the gift of time to make a wise choice

3. Fully protecting each other's minds, hearts, and bodies

4. Feeling totally cherished and respected

5. Maintaining full self-respect

6. Preserving the respect others have for you

7. Feeling secure because someone is fully committed to you

8. Feeling deeply loved because they were willing to give you 100 percent

9. Not feeling pressured

10. Not having to worry about pressuring or manipulating the other person

11. Not having to blame the other person for hurting you

12. Being free from guilt, shame, or regret about sex

13. Bringing no previous unhealthy sexual responses or images into your new bed

14. Deep trust that the other person has self-control

15. Respecting the other person for their self-control

16. Knowing that the other person can do what's hard

17. Knowing that the other person puts God first

18. Knowing that the other person would not ask you to do something that would put you at risk

19. Knowing that the other person loves all of you, not just parts

20. Appreciating that the other person isn't bringing diseases into your relationship

21. Not having to worry about the shame of unwed pregnancy

22. Feeling free to discuss problems because neither fears breakup

23. Not having to lie to, hide from, or avoid others

24. Having no regret

25. Increased self-confidence for having self-control

26. Being free from anger

27. Protecting your children from shame

28. Being able to model self-control and obedience for your future children

29. Creating a safe, whole environment for your children

30. Greatly decreased chance of divorce

31. Not having to deal with abortion, the courts, visitation, support, or custody issues

32. Protecting yourself from getting locked into an unhealthy relationship

33. Being able to give yourself totally to your spouse, with no memories of previous partners

34. Being able to please the other person without comparisons to previous partners getting in the way

35. Not having to worry that he/she is thinking of previous sex with someone else

36. Feeling right before God

37. Keeping a sense of unity between your mind, body, and spirit

38. A deep sense of peace and joy

* * *

You Can Choose True Love

Instead of looking at saving your best for last as a big "No!" think of it as the chance to be faithful right now to your soul mate, whom God has already created for you. Let's imagine you have already met that special person and fallen madly, deeply and passionately in love. He or she has had to go away for a while, where you cannot write or talk to each other. Would you remain true? Would you expect your soul mate to remain true?

Rebekah chose to save herself for Isaac, even though she never knew his name or when he would arrive. She trusted God for the time and place. Isaac and his family had carefully chosen and preserved the best gifts for Rebekah, even though they did not know where she was. Isaac and Rebekah chose to save the best they had to give in all areas for their soul mate, whether or not they knew who or where they were until the time was right.

The schools, the government, and the media continually hammer the message that today you have freedom of choice, and they are right. You have two choices:

- *Sex outside marriage:* false love, fear, anxiety, disease, disappointment, worry, guilt, shame, self-loathing, insecurity, manipulation, control, rejection, anger, frustration, loss, and lack of self-esteem.

- *Sex saved for marriage:* freedom, family, security, health, self-esteem, virtue, genuine love for one another, protection, provision, wholeness, happiness, mutual respect, trust, joy, and peace.

What will you choose?

What Does My Fear Say?

What if I am all alone or have no satisfaction or intimacy in my life? It will be terrible; it's not natural! I just can't do it!

What Does My Faith Say?

I can see how waiting has special rewards I never thought of, and how rushing brings heartache. I can choose to save the best for last as a gift to myself and my soul mate, and God will give me the grace to wait.

What Should I Remember?

- *I need to be aware of all areas of intimacy that can blind us or bind us.*
- *True love would never bring any type of harm into the relationship.*
- *Saving the best for last can reap rich rewards.*

❧ 12 ❧

Saying "I Do"

Bethuel sat outside his house with the other men, leaning up against the still-warm wall as the sun set. A rosy glow lingered along the purple hills as the evening sky draped slowly over the desert floor. It was quiet now, with only a distant camel's cry and a child's laugh.

"Father!" cried Rebekah as she raced around the corner, black braids flying, and a smile spread across her tanned, ten-year-old face. She plopped down on the ground next to Bethuel and curled up tightly under his arm. The scent of desert sage was strong as she breathed in the smell of her father.

He smiled. "What is it, my daughter?"

"Father," she said excitedly, "Laban taught me how to make a camel sit down to drink today. I did it all by myself!" She grinned proudly. "Tabas is older and he's still scared of camels!"

Her father laughed. "Rebekah, I am proud of you. You are already learning to be a good helpmate to your husband!"

Rebekah cocked her head slightly and asked seriously, "Father, when will I meet my husband? Will he be handsome?"

"The Lord will bring your husband when the time is right, my little one. Just be patient and continue to prepare yourself for him. When you are ready, he will come."

"But Father, I'm ready now!" All the men laughed, but Rebekah stuck out her lip. She didn't think it was funny.

Bethuel pulled his daughter close, lifted her chin, and looked into her eyes.

"Sweet one, Almighty God will take care of your husband. Perhaps he is preparing him for you right this very minute. For now, he wants you to become the best you can be in everything. Continue to be an obedient daughter; work hard, love your brothers and sisters, and don't forget to pray. The things you are learning now, even with those old camels, may lead your husband to you someday. Don't forget that."

Rebekah let out a deep sigh and sat quietly in her father's arms. Some days she just couldn't wait, but right now in her father's embrace, she felt as happy and loved as she could ever hope to be.

Saying "I Do" Right Now

I only imagined little Rebekah in her father's arms, but I have sometimes felt just like that, and I'm sure you have too: a little anxious, somewhat dreamy, but with my eyes hopefully on the future. We know years later little Rebekah's dreams eventually came true. If you read the rest of their love story, which unfolds like an adventurous romance novel, you'll see that after they married, Isaac and Rebekah had twin boys. But as their sons grew and life unfolded, their happily-ever-after included times of family heartache. Like every generation before us, we assume that our soul mate will bring us perfect happiness "forever and ever, amen." Sometimes, though, they don't. When those times come, we still need "our Father's arms" to wrap around us and let us know that a much greater love is always available to us.

Are you as anxious about meeting your soul mate as Rebekah was? No matter who he or she is; no matter when they show up, you can say, "I do" right now. You can make a commitment that you will love your soul mate all the days of your life, starting today. That means first saying "I don't" to others with whom you are already involved.

"That's hard," said one of the ladies in our DivorceCare group. She had been dating a man who was also recently divorced, and before they'd both properly healed from their previous relationships, they were sexually involved. She admitted she knew it was not right but she could not help herself. She'd chosen not to wait and now she was paying the price with the confusion and heartbreak of another failing romance.

We've already discussed how we often get into unhealthy relationships to avoid pain, but we also stay in them for the same reason. Most people stay with the wrong person for reasons that seem right, but ultimately only end up delaying the heartbreak. Are you familiar with these phrases? Have you repeated them yourself?

"She's better than nothing."

"He's better than nothing."

"I'm getting old!"

"I'll never find anyone else."

"I know I can help her change."

"I know with time he will grow up."

"We have too much history together."

"My biological clock is ticking."

"I don't want to be alone the rest of my life."

"But he loves me, and I don't want to hurt him."

"She taught me a lot; I'd feel guilty if I left."

"He takes care of me; I owe it to him."

"I can't afford to leave."

Yes, it is hard to leave an unhealthy relationship, especially when you've bonded on all the various levels of your being. All the more reason you should understand the depth to which marriage is meant to take you with only one special person. Are you in an unmarried relationship that needs to change? Have you decided that you don't want to give your heart away anymore until it's right? How do you say "I don't" when you already did? Just remember:

- The past is past. Today is the present. Today you can make a decision to approach relationships in a new way. This first requirement is coming to a place of faith in God and a trust that He can help meet your needs. Make God the center of your life. Maybe you're not there yet, but if you're sick of the same old cycle, *say "I do" to God's way of finding love.*

- You can ask God and the other person to forgive you for any hurt you have caused to yourself, to them, or to others, and pray for His wisdom and grace to begin a fresh start. *Say "I do" to a changed heart.*

- You can present your body to your soul mate even before you meet him or her. Rebekah saved her most precious self for one man. If you were married and your spouse had to go overseas to an unknown place for an unknown time, would you be willing to wait for their return? Would you be faithful? If you were the one leaving, wouldn't you expect your spouse to be faithful? Think of your soul mate as being "away" for now, but you can still be committed to him or her everyday. The careless or too-quick giving of your body to other people brings too much hurt in the end. It robs your future spouse of the private, perfect love that should belong only to him or her. No more memories made with mistaken identities. Present your body to your soul mate now, and protect it for his or her return. *Say "I do" to emotional and physical purity.*

- You can practice love on others. Rebekah obviously had developed a tender heart toward other people and was willing to love through service to a stranger. Real love is not just romance—it's healthy self-sacrifice. Your soul mate will need you to know how to love him or her, even when he or she is unlovable. If you can do that, what a gift you can bring to the relationship! One of the simplest steps to holiness is the discipline of showing God's love to others in all of life's daily details. A little love on a daily basis can go a long way. *Say" I do" to loving other people in the world.*

* * *

Practice loving the crabby clerk at the grocery store, because some days your soul mate will be crabby.

Practice letting the other car go first, because sometimes your soul mate will be pushy.

Practice smiling at the DMV when you don't feel like it, because your soul mate will need your smile like you need his or hers.

Practice saying "please" and "thank you" with the waitress, because your soul mate will deserve the same.

Practice allowing your friend to have the biggest or best because your soul mate also will need to know you love him or her more than that chocolate cake.

Practice patience with your neighbor's dog, because your soul mate will need you to overlook his or her barking, too.

Practice forgiving others when you are hurt, because your soul mate will need your forgiveness.

When God Says "I Do" to You

At some point in your life, it's important that you become aware that even a good soul mate relationship or marriage is no substitute for the Soul Mate for whom you ultimately were created. The marriage relationship between man and woman was designed by God to model how God loves you. The Lord is the Bridegroom who pursues you faithfully until you say, "I do." When you come to Him, He also says, "I do" to you. He is your ultimate protector, provider, and source of pure and true love. That's a lofty concept that is sometimes hard to understand until your mind and emotions mature and integrate with your spirit. But if you make a daily habit of turning to Him in the little things, you'll begin to see and hear his "I do's" all around you—like I did last year.

"Oh God," I cried quietly to myself, "not again." I was sitting in the passenger seat of a Cadillac Seville headed home from Los Angeles, where I'd spent a lovely day shopping with a man I was dating. We'd enjoyed each other's company for several months, but neither of us had brought up where our relationship was going. As evening fell, our casual conversation inched its way from the day's fun to the future, and he suddenly blurted out that he wasn't ready for a relationship (polite talk for "You're not the one"). I can take the end of a dating relationship if I can get up and walk or get into my car and drive away, but it's hell being trapped in *his* car an hour from home. It was especially hard because my husband had left me years before and now that old pain resurfaced, mixing itself with new rejection in a wave of sickening nausea.

How could I possibly sit there for one more hour, smelling his cologne and feeling his cool detachment? I wanted to scream. So I took a deep breath, let it out, and leaned my head away from him and against the car window. I closed my eyes and began to pray, "Not again, God. Please help me remember how valuable I am and how much I am loved by you. You love me . . . you love me . . . you love me . . . ," I chanted quietly to the hum of the engine. I breathed in and out slowly and tried to remember the big picture: that life will go on, and I will be fine. But the worry and grief wormed its way back to my mind and I whined just a little, "God, when is this rejection *ever* going to end?" I wanted to keep my eyes closed, but right then something made me open them. With my head still pressed against the glass, I peeked out into the pitch black of the desert night and in the blink of an eye I caught the message as we whizzed down the freeway past a single, lonely billboard. The sign had a dark background with large, white letters that read, "The Best Is Yet to Come." Nothing else, no picture, no product, no clue about what the marquis was advertising. I felt a chill go up my spine and a warmth flood my heart as I felt that message, in just that moment, had been from God to me. I smiled in the dark and, like little Rebekah, felt my Father's arms around me.

A week or so later, I was still trying to find contentment in my singleness and to not obsess about being dumped. I had to run an errand on a side of town I rarely frequent and decided, on the spur of the moment, to stop in at Albertson's grocery store for a gallon of nonfat milk. As I walked back to my car, I noticed out of the corner of my eye a young man quickly approaching me. I remembered my LAPD "Self Defense for Women" class and quickly turned to face him, milk in my hands, and my car key ready to gouge out his eyes. He was young, handsome, and grinning from ear to ear. Oh brother, I thought, another grocery store pickup. Next he'll probably ask me what my sign is. Instead, he stopped, held his hand straight out and said, "Here. These are for you!" As I stood ready to karate chop him, he put a large bouquet of beribboned flowers into my hand, turned, and walked away. I stood there in shock, smelling the flowers, and waiting for the hidden agenda, but by the time I looked up he'd disappeared. I threw the milk in the trunk, laid the flowers on the front seat, and put the car in reverse before it hit me. "Wow! These are from *you*, God," I thought happily. "*Thank you!*"

Like a faithful and understanding spouse, first he sent me a reassuring love note on the billboard, and now he'd sent his messenger to deliver flowers. What would be next?

Do you remember my girlfriend Shirley who I mentioned in the introduction? The one who tried to set me up with the spy? Well, I'd agreed to one more blind date and was waiting for my doorbell to ring, thinking *here I go again . . . another boring date. I wonder what this guy will be like?* Suddenly I was overcome with a warm flush and that familiar tingle in my spine, and I almost heard God whisper tenderly in my ear, "Rose, when are you going to realize that I AM all you will ever need?"

I tuned in and continued to listen to him whisper sweet nothings in my ear as my mind was flooded with thoughts spilling over each other of how much God loves me, how he'll never leave me, and how he has wonderful things in store for me each and every day. It didn't matter after that if my date turned out to be a dud or not, I already had a love-note, flowers, and sweet talk from Another. I went on my date with a heart open to a much greater love than one night's expectations. Dinner was fine, the company was okay, but more than that, I got my perspective back. With each year that goes by, my friendship with singleness is deepening into love.

The Three Stones

Imagine you are standing at the edge of a rushing river, where the water is composed of all the pulls and pushes of life, swirling with "I wants," "I needs," and "I have-to-haves." You look out and see a loving God on the other side, and all you want to do is walk out and be with Him, but the things you pursue are in the way, threatening to pull you under. In reality, God is here with you right now, but it's the imperfect human mind and emotions that need to cross over and close the gap.

Sometimes we feel further away from Him than at other times; sometimes the river might seem like an ocean. But if you want to get from where you are now to that place where your mind and emotions can know and feel His love, you can jump across on three special stepping-stones. You can keep these pebbles in your pocket and take them wherever you go and use them anytime. No matter if the water is a raging river or a babbling brook, just throw them out before you, watch them grow to hold you, and take three steps back into His arms:

The First Stone

Remember who you are. You are a pure spirit created by God, yet living in this body just a short while. All your needs, wants, and earthly desires, even for a soul mate, will someday pass away. You were created in His image to spend eternity with Him in the presence of His pure love. It doesn't matter who you are or what you've done in the past, you're precious and deeply loved by the Lord. This daily act of remembering who you are, remembering who He is, and remembering His love and promises for you will start to get you across the river. Now reach out and take God's hand—for He is the One to bridge the gap and, ultimately, help you across. Get the big picture.

The Second Stone

Rejoice in God's creation. Every day take a look around you at the things you think you want badly. The beautiful place you wish you could live, the yard full of flowers, the gorgeous clothes, the sparkle of jewels, the laughter of children, the things you want but can't afford, the love of a family member, the career you pursue, the concert you want to attend, and even the deep love of a soul mate. All of these, which were created, should serve as a reminder of something greater. Taste, touch, see, hear, and smell all the delights and joys of creation and rejoice in their pleasure. But remember that they are only a pale imitation of their Creator, a mere reflection of Him. They can never bring the full and unending pleasure He can.

The Third Stone

Remove yourself slowly. After r*emembering* who you are and *rejoicing* in the delights that await you, begin to *remove* yourself emotionally from those urgent needs and wants that control you. Removing your heart from things doesn't mean moving to Tibet or joining a convent; it's an everyday emotional detachment that says, "I'd like this, and I'm willing to pursue it if it's good for me, but I'm also willing to do without it. I remember the bigger picture; I rejoice in what I have had in the past and what I will have in the future, but I am letting go of the fierce 'I wants' in my life."

You'll always want and need earthly pleasures and delights; it's normal and healthy to aspire to goals and to dream dreams, especially for a soul mate. In themselves, these things may not be bad for you, but your "have-to-have" attitudes can drown you. Your emotional attachment to the things you want may keep your eyes away from God. As long as you want things more than you want to be close to God, you'll be flooded with fear, worry, anxiety, or anger. A habitual focus on the silvery "I needs" that swim in the stream of life can cause you to lose your balance, fall in, and be carried away. In fixing your gaze on the love that awaits you, and stepping out on *remembering*, *rejoicing*, and *removing*, you can close the watery gap between being controlled and being free . . . between stressful anxiety and loving peace.

- In remembering you practice your *faith*,
- In rejoicing you embrace your *hope* and,
- In removing yourself emotionally from things and coming closer to God, you move to *love*.

I know my search for a soul mate (like yours) is the beginning of recognizing how much I need to give and receive love—that I was made by Love for Love. I hope that in your journey for a soul mate that you'll remember what Eliezer did when he asked for help. Always remember that

God, the One who loves you and wants the best for you, will help you on your quest.

He knows and remembers your name.

He listens to every word you utter.

He wants to provide for you and meet your needs.

He wants to help you do what you cannot do alone.

He's given you his love letters when you need direction or encouragement.

He makes good advice available and sends help when you need it.

He wants to walk with you and share your burdens.

He brings light to lead your way and dark to give you rest.

He brings you flowers in the spring and sets fruit before you in the fall.

He is always there for you, whenever you call.

He will lift you up when you're weary.

He will dry your tears when you grieve.

His ways are unchanging.

He is always faithful.

He is holy, righteous, and pure.

He wants to give you endless love and deep satisfaction.

He never will leave or forsake you.

He is the ancient of days, the King of Kings, and Lord of Lords.

He is the First and Last, the Beginning and End.

May you come to know Him and love Him even more in your search for a soul mate.

Prayer for a Soul Mate

In my search for love, please send
A helper, guide, or trusted friend.
Show me, too, how I should grow
And give me grace to make it so.

I'll seek a mate who's pure and true
Please help me stay the same way, too.
Increase my faith, but let me see
Some special sign You send to me.

Open up my eyes and ears
To ask and learn, despite my fears.
Grant me patience that I may wait,
Trusting You for my soul mate.

Grant me courage to save my best,
Guard my heart from all the rest.
And when at last I know it's right,
Keep both of us within Your sight.

I thank you, God, for all you do
And may my search bring me *to You*.

Endnotes

Chapter 2

1. Pam Stenzel, *Sex, Love and Relationships* (Worcester, PA: Vision Video, Inc., 1998).

2. David Popenoe, Ph.D. and Barbara Dafoe Whitehead, Ph.D., *Rutgers University National Marriage Project*, http://marriage.rutgers.edu/TEXTSOOU2001.htm.

3. Oprah Winfrey, "Family: Now More Than Ever," *O, the Oprah Magazine* (December 2001), 33.

4. Thomas Moore, *Soul Mates: Honoring the Mysteries of Love and Relationship* (New York: Harper Collins, 1994), xvii.

5. Ann Landers, *The Desert Sun* (18 January 2002), D3.

6. Cheryl Wetzstein, "Singles Desperate to Avoid Divorce, Find Soul Mate," *The Washington Times* (18-24 June 2001), 1.

7. Maria Elena Fernandez, "Soul(MATE) Searching," *Los Angeles Times* (17 June 2001), E1.

Chapter 4

1. Dr. Bruce H. Wilkinson, *The Prayer of Jabez: Breaking Through to the Blessed Life* (Sisters, Oregon: Multnomah Publishers, 2000), 24.

2. William Gibson, *The Miracle Worker* (New York: Bantam Books, 1956).

Chapter 5

1. Dr. Neil Clark Warren, Ph.D., *Finding the Love of Your Life: Ten Principles for Choosing the Right Marriage Partner* (Wheaton, Illinois: Tyndale House Publishing, 1992), 145.

2. Rose Sweet, *A Woman's Guide to Healing the Heartbreak of Divorce* (Peabody, Maine: Hendrickson, 2001).

3. Rula Razek, "Shall We Meet 'f2f'?," *USA Today Weekend* (20-22 July 2001), 6.

4. Quoted from article by Shauna Scott Rhone, "Tips to help steer singles into 2002," *The Desert Sun* (30 December 2001), C3.

Chapter 6

1. Jan Denise Soroka, "Perfect Love Will Find You," *The Desert Sun* (23 July 2001), D1.

2. Dr. Gary Lawrence, *Rejection Junkies* (Phoenix: GLS Publishing, 1996).

3. Florence and Marita Littauer, *Getting Along with Almost Anybody—The Complete Personality Book* (Grand Rapids: Fleming H. Revell, 1998), 325.

4. Dr. Patricia Allen and Sandra Harmon, *Getting To I Do—The Secret To Doing Relationships Right* (New York: Avon Books, 1994), 25.

Chapter 7

1. Dr. Randy Carlson, "Kids on Call," *Parent Talk Magazine* (March 2001), 6.

2. Dr. Gary Lawrence, *Rejection Junkies* (Phoenix, Ariz.: GLS Publishing, 1996).

3. Neil Clark Warren, Ph.D., *How to Know If Someone Is Worth Pursuing in Two Dates or Less,* (Nashville, Tenn.: Thomas Nelson, 1999), 52-53.

4. Ibid.

Chapter 10

1. Pamela Paul, *The Starter Marriage and the Future of Matrimony* (New York: Random House, 2002), 4.

2. Bruce Horovitz, "24/7 Almost a Way of Life," *USA Today* (1 August 2001), 1B.

3. David Popenoe, Ph.D. and Barbara Dafoe Whitehead, Ph.D., *Rutgers University National Marriage Project*, http://marriage.rutgers.edu/TEXTSOOU2001.htm.

Chapter 11

1. Laura Vanderkam, "Hookups Starve the Soul," *USA Today* (26 July 2001), 15A.

2. Ecclesiastes 1:9.